THE USA IN
WORLD WAR 2

THE USA IN WORLD WAR 2

THE PACIFIC THEATER

DOUGLAS WELSH

Bison Books Limited

First published in the UK by
Bison Books Ltd
4 Cromwell Place
London SW7

Copyright © 1982 by Bison Books Ltd

Produced by Bison Books Ltd

ISBN 0-86124-052-9

Printed in Hong Kong

CONTENTS

Contents

1. Approach to Pearl Harbor — 6
2. The Japanese Offensive — 14
3. The Tide Turns — 20
4. Pacific Sideshows — 30
5. New Guinea and the Solomons — 34
6. Across the Central Pacific — 38
7. Return to the Philippines — 47
8. Iwo Jima and Okinawa — 54
9. The Eclipse of the Rising Sun — 60
   Index — 64

1 APPROACH TO PEARL HARBOR

Above left: President Roosevelt warns against Axis aggression in a September 1941 broadcast.
Above: Admiral Shimada, Japanese Navy Minister in 1941.

Above: Admiral Yamamoto planned the attack on Pearl Harbor.
Right and below right: Scenes of devastation in the aftermath of the Pearl Harbor strike.

As the war in Europe escalated in 1941 the United States watched with growing concern. President Franklin Delano Roosevelt was committed to the Allied cause and expected that the United States would be drawn into the conflict. However it would be in a different hemisphere that the United States would first mobilize its military might. American involvement would begin and end in the Pacific against Japan.

The actual event which precipitated America's war with Japan was of course the attack on Pearl Harbor on 7 December 1941. President Roosevelt and his staff were aware of the sensitivity of American relations with Japan but they had not fully understood the most recent developments prior to 7 December. There was ominous warning of the possibilities of confrontation which were not publicly known but which must be analyzed.

Japan's military leaders, particularly Admiral Yamamoto, realized that Japan was not capable of fighting an extended war with the United States. Neither the Japanese military nor industry, though extremely competent, could hope to compete with America once the United States was fully mobilized. Yamamoto had spent time studying in the US and recognized the potential will, strength and determination of the American people. After Pearl Harbor he would refer to the United States as the 'sleeping giant' which the belligerent Japanese policy had awakened but had not destroyed.

However, before Pearl Harbor, America was dormant as it had been prior to World War I. Its isola-

tionist policy had grown more deep rooted. There were four primary reasons for the strength of the isolationist doctrine. First the United States had been disillusioned by the results of World War I when neither peace, democracy nor disarmament had been achieved. The dream that World War I was the 'war to end all wars' was shattered so completely in the aftermath that the American people lost faith in the alleged principles for which the war was fought. The overwhelming opinion was clearly that no more American blood should be spilled in the petty quarrels of the European powers. In the late 1930's that sentiment was applied to the developing confrontation between Japan and China. Second, though related to the first point, was the failure of the League of Nations as an effective tool of peace. Although the United States had not joined the League it was disturbed and disheartened by the League's inability to influence nations' activities or put a rein on the aggressive postures taken by Germany, Italy or Japan. This reconfirmed the American opinion that the League members did not truly want lasting peace. The United States responded with an attitude that portrayed a lack of concern for the actions of other world governments, so long as they did not affect the United States. Third, the United States found security in the Atlantic and Pacific Oceans which separated it from other

belligerent nations. If Canada, Central and South America were kept on friendly terms the United States believed it had nothing to worry about. The continental United States had not been successfully invaded since the War of 1812 and the brief Spanish-American War had shown the enormous difficulties of attempting to transport troops and materiel for that purpose to North America. Finally, the ultimate disillusion came when in 1934 the United States Senate Investigating Committee revealed that bankers and other monetary institutions and individuals had amassed large profits during World War I and that the money lent by the United States to the Allies had directly influenced American military involvement in that war. The thought that some had actually become rich on the blood of American soldiers horrified the American people and promoted a strong pacifist ideal.

The goal of strict neutrality was reinforced by legislation passed which opposed or prohibited involvement of the United States in European or Asian affairs. The Neutrality Laws prohibited the shipment of arms or munitions to warring nations and made it illegal for Americans to travel on vessels of warring nations or enter war zones. In 1937 the President was given the authority to itemize non-military goods which could be sold to belligerent parties on a 'cash and carry' basis. This no credit policy was intended to

prevent the United States from entering war to assure the recoupment of its investments.

Although the pacifist argument was strong many Americans were dissatisfied with the position. They urged that the United States as a superpower should take a more prominent role in world politics and events. A belief in the moral duty of America to stand for individual rights and to be the protector of victims of aggression emerged. This concept was well favored by President Roosevelt. Although the United States had pulled itself from the Depression the economic effect of the sale of materiels abroad could result in total recovery. The President considered it sufficient to quarantine nations which were classified by the United States as overt aggressors. The neutralist-isolationist position was stronger. Even in December 1937 when Japanese planes bombed and strafed the American gunboat *Panay* and three American oil tankers on the Yangtze River in China, killing and wounding several Americans, that position did not waver. In fact public opinion polls indicated that 60 percent of Americans favored withdrawing from China, thus removing the United States from the possibility of involvement in the conflict between China and Japan. It was also urged that the United States accept Japan's apologies and offers of compensation and forget the incident.

By 1938 the volatile world situation had convinced Roosevelt that it was only a matter of time before the United States would be forced to defend itself. The American people and Congress were fundamentally opposed to the institution of an armament program, but the President felt compelled to begin building America's readiness. He requested greatly increased funds from Congress to help strengthen the navy. While publicly committed to peace and neutrality Roosevelt considered Germany, Italy and Japan as nothing more than 'international bandits.' His Secretary of the Interior Harold L Ickes went so far as to publicly label Hitler as a 'maniac.' While the Roosevelt Administration 'talked tough' its hands were bound by the unwillingness of the American people or Congress to support what might be construed as an aggressive posture.

Throughout 1939 the President called for negotiations to settle the European and Asian differences, but at the same time he urged Congress to repeal the 1935 and 1937 neutrality legislation. In the fall of 1939 modifications to the Neutrality Laws were passed and Roosevelt immediately began to swing America's limited strength behind France and Great Britain. In November the 'cash and carry' arrangements were extended to allow weapons and munitions to be sent to those European nations which would resist Hitler and his allies. However there was to be no direct American involvement and in October the Panama Conference gave clear warning that America and its Western Hemisphere allies were prepared to assert

their positions against aggression of any kind.

By May 1940 the war in Europe was fully engaged. The United States hastened to adopt defensive measures during the summer and autumn of 1940 but there was an overriding sentiment that unless attacked the United States should remain neutral regardless of the European situation. The 'no credit' policy was also set aside when FDR introduced his Lend-Lease proposal. In March 1941 Congress approved the concept, appropriating $7,000,000,000 for ships, aircraft, tanks, munitions and other materiel which the Allies might require. When in June 1941 Germany invaded the USSR, Roosevelt promptly extended Lend-Lease to the Soviet Union. Although Roosevelt focussed attention on Europe, by July Japan had occupied French Indo-China. Caught relatively off guard by the developing crisis in the Far East, Roosevelt abruptly reacted with legislation against Japan. All Japanese assets in the United States were frozen. Sanctions prohibiting the transfer of manufactured goods and raw materials to Japan were instituted.

These were severe blows to Japan as its own resources, including petroleum products, machine tools, iron and steel, were inadequate to its expansion needs. Japan accepted the actions as hostile and reacted by freezing the largest American asset holdings in Japan. American-Japanese trade was brought to a halt. Friction between the two governments prompted Roosevelt to extend the Lend-Lease program in August 1941 to benefit China, with whom the Japanese had been in conflict since 1937.

Japan was faced with a critical dilemma. To continue to expand the Empire Japan had embarked on a strategy of absorbing those Far East areas which were rich in the industrial and agricultural raw materials which she lacked. The shift in American policy meant that the Japanese would have to act swiftly to neutralize the American power base in the Far East. Japan was

negotiations had provided the time necessary for Japan's leaders to formulate and set in motion their military strategy against the United States. Before the final message could be properly delivered to the American government on 7 December 1941 Japan attacked the US base at Pearl Harbor.

America was appalled at the duplicity exhibited by Japan in committing an act of war while peaceful negotiations were in progress, an action which was exacerbated by two circumstances: war had not been declared and no advance warning had been given. It is the latter point which must be clarified, for there was indeed warning that Japan intended to extend its efforts in the Pacific. Throughout November and the first days of December American monitoring stations in the Pacific intercepted Japanese marine radio transmissions. It became evident that Japan's fleets were

Top left: Gunners aboard the *Panay* fire at attacking Japanese planes.
Above left: The *Panay* sinks after the Japanese attack, 12 December 1937. The Stars and Stripes can be clearly seen on the awning beside the mast.
Above right: Admiral Kimmel (center) pictured with his senior staff officers in 1941. Kimmel was dismissed soon after Pearl Harbor and Nimitz became Commander in Chief, Pacific Fleet.

compelled to act but realized that time would have to be bought for its military leaders to prepare a response for the United States. In November 1941 Japan sent a peace mission to Washington to enumerate the problems which would have to be resolved so that, in the words of the Japanese government, 'the United States and Japan would not be propelled into war.' There were three fundamental Japanese demands: the release of Japanese assets, the supply of petroleum products to Japan and a halt to aid to China. Proposals and counterproposals were made. Finally a document was issued by the Japanese government announcing that further negotiations were futile and that the United States clung to an impractical principle, demonstrating no desire to resolve the situation. The

moving on Hong Kong, Indo-China and Malaysia with hostile intent. However, the Japanese Carrier Groups I and II, which were the pride of the Japanese Navy and contained the six most powerful carriers, could not be located. It was a paradox. Intelligence agencies realized that the carrier groups would have to be part of any major offensive, yet the silence seemed to indicate that the groups were in Japanese home waters. By 1 December the Commander in Chief of the US Pacific Fleet, Admiral Husband E Kimmel, had decided that the carriers could not be in Japanese waters but there was little evidence of their actual position. There was of course the possibility of an attack on Pearl Harbor. The vulnerability of the base there had been illustrated in maneuvers and studies at American military academies. However, Kimmel believed that a more probable Japanese target was the Philippines. Although both the Pacific Fleet Command and informed Washington sources were aware of the possibility of an attack on Pacific installations, little preparatory action was taken. In retrospect the inactivity of the American command makes it appear as though the Pacific Fleet was being sacrificed as a means to draw the United States into war.

At 0700 hours Hawaii time on 7 December 1941 an American radar station on the northern coast of Oahu Island detected a large number of aircraft 139 miles north of the island. Those aircraft belonged to Vice-Admiral Nagumo's Fleet and their destination was Pearl Harbor. The subsequent events sealed the fate of both the Pacific Fleet and the United States. The men assigned to the Oahu radar station had little experience and although the operators reported the sighting, valuable time was wasted as they checked and rechecked their systems. Initially they believed that the radar equipment was malfunctioning, as it had a reputation of doing. When they were satisfied that the equipment was operating properly their information was relayed to the primary information center at Pearl Harbor. The young officer who received the message was unsure of the proper response. It was a Sunday morning and there was no one to ask for guidance. Checking his records, the lieutenant finally ordered the operators to disregard the sighting as a flight of American B-17 bombers was scheduled to be arriving from the States. The aircraft monitored by the radar unit were approaching from the wrong direction for a flight from the United States, but the possibility that there was a malfunction temporarily sufficed to allay suspicions. It is important to note that an extended period of time elapsed during these communications as the radar personnel had to hike several miles down a mountain to reach the nearest telephone and relay their information.

Thirty minutes later 183 Japanese aircraft converged on Oahu from three directions. The first group flew from a westerly seaward direction. The second

Above: The destroyers *Cassin* and *Downes* and the battleship *Pennsylvania* were in dock when the Japanese attack was made. The *Pennsylvania* escaped with comparatively minor damage.
Right: Rescue teams stand by near the burning *West Virginia*. The *West Virginia* was raised and refitted for service later in the war.
Below: The maps show the course of the Japanese attacks and their targets in the fleet anchorage. The vital oil storage tanks shown in the detailed plan were, however, left untouched.

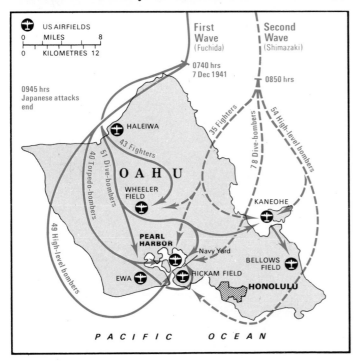

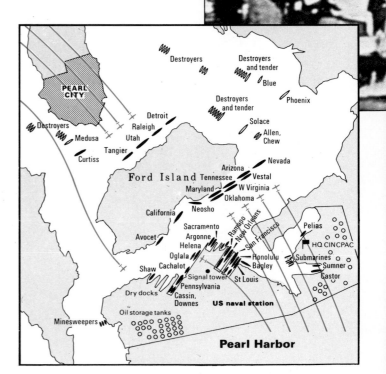

10

approached from due west and the third crossed the island for attacks on inland targets. A second wave of aircraft attacked from an eastern seaward route. At 0800 hours the attack began, catching the American base completely by surprise. Within the first 30 minutes the battleship *Arizona* had exploded, the *West Virginia* had sunk, and the *Oklahoma* had capsized. The Japanese attack produced horror stories that shocked the world. Descriptions of survivors told of Pearl Harbor 'raining sailors' as the *Arizona* exploded and tossed its crewmen into the air. There were descriptions of the inferno which engulfed the bay as oil spread flames across the water. There were even those who spoke of seeing the faces of Japanese pilots as their aircraft flew low to strafe or merely to

bank over the harbor to inspect the damage they had caused. The inland assault was as devastating. Japanese air attacks destroyed American aircraft on Wheeler, Hickam, Ford Island and Kaneohe airfields. The fleet and airfields attempted to mount a desperate defense but it served no effective purpose.

At 1000 hours the Japanese vanished as suddenly as they had appeared. In the presence of his staff Admiral Kimmel removed his epaulets, symbolizing the loss of his fleet and certainly his command position as a result of the disaster. By afternoon inspections revealed that eight battleships, three cruisers, three destroyers and eight auxiliary vessels were damaged or destroyed. The four airfields were severely damaged with 96 of the 231 aircraft destroyed. Only seven of the remaining aircraft were considered fit to fly as the others had suffered varying degrees of damage. Casualty reports indicated that at least 3500 American military personnel and civilians had been lost.

The Japanese initially believed their operation to be a complete success. However, their victory was momentary and seriously flawed. The American aircraft carriers, which had been Admiral Yamamoto's primary objectives when he conceived the plan, were away from the base when it was attacked. The Japanese submarines which had been launched against the harbor had failed to reach their targets. Of the naval vessels attacked, only two battleships and two destroyers were incapacitated permanently, having been sunk or destroyed. Moreover, the loss of the American battleships produced an effect that the Japanese had not anticipated. The American naval command was compelled to revise its strategy. The carriers were to become the ultimate weapon in the Pacific, replacing the battleship forever as the core of the US Navy. The loss, if only temporary of so many naval vessels also created a new concept in the priorities of military theorists. Old ideas of brute force in naval warfare would be replaced by the innovative approach of imaginative commanders in the Pacific. The Japanese had also erred politically. The nature of the attack welded the American people into a common front. Congress was outraged and rallied behind the President in his call for war. Roosevelt's speech proclaiming, 'Pearl Harbor will live forever as a day of infamy,' roused the American people in the call to arms. Japan would indeed enjoy a period of victorious advance in the Pacific but would soon realize the full impact of having angered 'the sleeping giant.'

Above: News of the Pearl
Harbor attack reaches the
continental United States.
Above left: A wrecked B-17
Flying Fortress bomber on
Bellows Field, Oahu on
7 December 1941.
Left: The old *Omaha* Class light
cruiser USS *Raleigh* under
repair after the Pearl Harbor
attack.
Right: The remains of a P-40
fighter seen on Wheeler Field,
Oahu.

2 THE JAPANESE OFFENSIVE

Only two of the eight US battleships in Pearl Harbor were total losses. All the others were repaired for service with bombardment forces later in the war.

The strike at Pearl Harbor, although uppermost in the minds of the American people, was not the only Japanese operation being implemented in the Pacific. Although the point is subject to debate, the United States would almost certainly have found its position in the Pacific extremely difficult had the Pearl Harbor attack not taken place. As it was, even though the primary Japanese targets, the carriers, had escaped destruction while on maneuvers, the United States was not prepared for war against Japan.

The Japanese need and desire for a cheap resource pool was the driving force behind their grasp for power and territory in the Far East. The acquisition of those resources would enable Japan to increase the pace of its industrial revolution and give it influence in controlling markets in peacetime. The elimination of American might in the Pacific was the most direct course to a rapid peace settlement and the redirection of Japan's industries from war to peace production. To pursue its goals, Japan had to expand its power sphere in two interdependent directions. First the conquest of Southeast Asia, the Dutch East Indies, Java and other similar regions must be accomplished to gain access to their mineral and agricultural resources. Then Japan had to eliminate the Western European and American military presence and throw a protective ring around its newly acquired territories. The defensive ring was dependent on the building and holding of island fortresses in the Pacific. The original concept suggested a circular pattern of defense from Wake Island to the Marshall Islands and the Bismarck Archipelago. The Japanese believed that any territory north of Wake Island and the Marshall Islands automatically lay in their sphere of influence and should belong to Japan forever. Their primary goal was therefore to conquer the perimeter islands as quickly as possible.

While Pearl Harbor was being attacked, the Japanese Navy was striking at the Philippines, Guam, Wake Island and other island objectives. The United States and its allies were awed at the speed with which the Japanese were able to attain their goals. By 10 December the Philippines had been invaded and Guam had been captured. On 23 December Wake Island succumbed to overwhelming odds after a brave resistance. On Christmas Day, Hong Kong, Britain's most valuable Far East port was lost. It became obvious that if the United States hoped to launch a productive campaign against Japan it would have to do so simultaneously on five major fronts. American military leaders had long considered an operation such as Japan was successfully waging to be impossible, thus the American military position in the island region was poorly placed and inadequate. The five fronts would include Wake and Guam, Hong Kong, the Philippines, Malaysia and Singapore, and the Dutch East Indies. The humiliation of the United States' and European colonial forces in those early days caused many to question whether the Japanese advance could possibly be stopped.

Of the five fronts originally considered, the battle for the Philippines was the most heated and of longest duration. These islands were not essential to Japan's economic goal but the elimination of the American military and political presence there fulfilled the second of Japan's objectives. If the Philippines were not conquered, the Americans could use them as a staging site, posing an obvious threat to Japan's power sphere. The Philippines were the point of strongest American military influence and defeat for the United States on those islands would have a grave effect on the morale of the American people. The United States had also recruited a large Philippine Army in previous years under the command and guidance of General Douglas MacArthur, America's most senior ranking officer who had been attached to the service of the Philippine government for that express purpose.

The Japanese opened their attack on the Philippines at the American B-17 bomber base at Clark Field, north of Manila. However, MacArthur had placed the Philippines on alert status and the initial Japanese raids found the airfield deserted. Later on 8 December (because of the intervention of the International Dateline 8 December, Philippines time was equivalent to 7 December, Pearl Harbor time) the B-17 squadron returned to prepare for bombing raids on Formosa. A second wave of Japanese aircraft caught the B-17s on the ground, destroying half the bombers and 80 other aircraft. This virtually eliminated American air power in the area. The main Japanese landings on the west coast of Luzon, the primary island of the Philippine chain, did not occur until 22 December although initial landings were made on the 10th. Japan committed its entire Fourteenth Army to the assault, but for almost two weeks American and Philippine forces offered stiff resistance. Japanese reinforcements had to be added to the offensive, which prevented their planned deployment elsewhere. Finally 106,000 American and Philippine troops and civilians were driven back to the Bataan Peninsula on Manila Bay. These numbers were far more than the area could feasibly support but they stubbornly refused to surrender. The location proved impossible to resupply or reinforce yet for three months the allied troops fought bitterly against the Japanese. In February 1942 President Roosevelt and his Chief of Staff General George Marshall ordered General MacArthur to leave his army at Bataan and assume command of American forces in Australia from whence to prepare a defense against the Japanese. MacArthur, whose service seniority and personal character would prove difficult to control throughout the war, balked at the orders. However on 12 March he reluctantly left the Philippines vowing, 'I shall return.' His successor General Jonathan Wainwright took command as the Japanese intensified their operations. From 3–8 April the Japanese renewed their attacks on Bataan. The American and Philippine forces resisted but they were starving and exhausted and were forced to surrender. General Wainwright

moved to the fortified island of Corregidor to establish a new defensive position with those who could escape from Bataan to join him.

When Bataan fell the Japanese showed no mercy to their defeated foe. They drove their American and Philippine captives 65 miles to prison camps on the island. The incident would become known as the 'Bataan Death March.' It is estimated that 25,000 died in the final hours of the battle and during that march. Another 22,000 would die at the camps in less than two months. The Bataan Death March would become a rallying issue in the United States as emotional as the cry 'Remember Pearl Harbor.' When General Wainwright and his men, through exhaustion of their supplies and ammunition, were forced to surrender on Corregidor they faced no better treatment. Although it had taken four months, the Japanese had destroyed the American presence in the Philippines and had gained a crucial victory in the expansion of their empire. They had also gained an infamous reputation as a vicious, inhumane enemy who was to be hated and ultimately destroyed. They had attempted a massive propaganda campaign in the Philippines. Leaflets, radio broadcasts and loudspeakers on the battlefields urged the Philippine military and civilians to stop fighting for their 'Yankee Masters' and join the Japanese in their goal of establishing 'Asia for the Asiatics.' The smallest minority of Philippine nationals responded to the propaganda

Above: A Douglas Dauntless dive bomber is given the signal to take off from its carrier. It carries a 1000-pound bomb.

Above: Admiral Ernest J King, Commander in Chief, US Navy. Top: Admiral Chester Nimitz, CINCPAC, 1941–45.

while the majority fought beside the Americans until the end, then marched with them to the death camps rather than serve the Japanese. This attitude brought harsh reprisals against the people of the Philippines and the frustration of the Japanese goaded them into some of their most abhorrent and foolish treatment of prisoners. The terror that Japan's military leaders had thought to instill in the soft and decadent Western peoples through their atrocities in the Philippines would backfire. Instead it would be channeled into a vengeful, retaliatory determination in the American people and their allies.

In December, while the early battles in the Philippines were being fought, Admiral Ernest J King took control of the US Navy while Admiral Chester W Nimitz was appointed Commander in Chief of the Pacific Fleet. Both men were excellent choices for their positions. They were men of great vision, understanding the necessary changes of naval warfare in the Pacific and recognizing the role of the carrier and the airplane in the war effort. Together they began to forge American strength around this precept. But in the opening days of the war America was on the defensive. A small number of carrier aircraft was able to harass the outer perimeter of the Japanese advance

but their effects were minimal. Pressure was being felt throughout the Far East. British and Dutch colonies fell rapidly. In February a small fleet commanded by Dutch Rear-Admiral Karl Doorman met a Japanese fleet in the Java Sea and was destroyed in the battle bearing that name. The cruiser USS *Houston* was among the ships lost in the Java Sea and the Allied naval presence in the area was eliminated.

It was then that the Allied commanders decided that an affirmative action of some sort must take place to lift the morale of the American people. Admirals King and Nimitz and Air Corps General Henry 'Hap' Arnold devised a daring scheme. Their military objective was limited. Their primary goal was to provide propaganda for use against the Japanese. It was to be a unique attempt to throw the Japanese into a state of confusion and loss of confidence with regard to the strategic concept of a defensive perimeter around their empire. The idea was to launch American bombers from aircraft carriers to strike at the Japanese Home Islands. After the strike they would proceed to bases in China where the bombers would become the property of the Chinese for further use against Japan. Lieutenant Colonel James H Doolittle was chosen to lead the 16 B-25 bombers on this mission. On 2 April 1942 the carrier USS *Hornet* which had left San Francisco carrying the bombers rendezvoused with the other ships in the force. On 18 April a Japanese patrol vessel was sighted while the *Hornet* was still 700 miles from Japan. Rather than abort the mission the bombers were launched, 200 miles ahead of their scheduled departure point. The Japanese patrol boat did report the sighting of the carrier but the Japanese High Command reacted with the assumption that the American vessel carried normal carrier aircraft, not long range bombers. They estimated that there would be at least 24 hours delay before aircraft could be launched, which gave the Japanese ample time to react. They were thus taken by complete surprise when some four hours later American bombers struck Tokyo, Kobe and Nagoya. Although the raid was relatively successful, inclement weather and the longer flight caused many of the pilots to become disoriented. Most ran out of fuel and were forced to crash land in China. Seventy-one of the 80 crew members of the mission survived to be returned eventually to rejoin the US forces. On 25 April the *Hornet* received a jubilant reception in Pearl Harbor and America celebrated its first major blow struck against the Japanese.

The Tokyo raid was an enormous boost to American morale. When reports on the raid were released the US Government claimed that the aircraft had been launched from a secret island base known as Shangri-la. Although the Japanese military leaders knew that the raid had been sent from an American carrier they were not prepared to admit to the Japanese people that the United States had the carrier potential to bring the war to the Japanese homeland. In fact to some degree the raid served as a perfect excuse for the Japanese leaders to expand the defensive perimeter which had been established. That perimeter could be expanded with the assertion that further elimination of American 'secret bases' was essential to the security of Japan. The Japanese commanders had been encouraged by the ease with which the initial objectives had been met. They decided to extend their sphere of influence as far north as the Aleutian Islands then to Midway Island, the Gilbert and Ellice Islands and the New Hebrides, Fiji, New Caledonia, the Solomons, Papua, and finally Port Moresby in New Guinea. This would give Japan control of the entire western Pacific and would isolate Australia and China from the aid being given them by the United States. However promising the situation appeared to the Imperial Command, they would find themselves overreaching their capabilities. Although not apparent to them the strategy would prove to be one step too far for Japan to maintain an effective military force.

As Japanese forces swung through the southern Solomon Islands and Papua they met minimal resistance, but as they turned toward Port Moresby the situation began to alter. The Japanese strike force consisted of two carriers which had played a primary role in the attack on Pearl Harbor, the *Zuikaku* and the *Shokaku*. Both had experienced commanders and crews and were considered the elite of the Japanese Navy. Their mission was to aid the invasion of Port Moresby and counter any effort that the United States or its allies might make to hamper that invasion. The Japanese escort carrier *Shoho* was also present to provide direct air support to the landing.

American Intelligence had for some time been breaking the Japanese secret military code and knew of the invasion intent and objective. In response the Navy sent a strike force of two large carriers, the *Yorktown* and the *Lexington*, five heavy cruisers and eleven destroyers commanded by Rear-Admiral Frank J Fletcher to the area. A small support fleet commanded by Rear-Admiral Sir John Crace of the Royal Australian Navy accompanied Fletcher and consisted of three heavy cruisers, two Australian and one American. Fletcher's orders were simple and direct, 'stop the invasion of Port Moresby.' The Japanese and American fleets would come to blows in the Coral Sea. The most curious aspect of the impending battle was that throughout its course neither the Japanese nor the Allied fleets would ever have direct visual contact with their opponents. The entire battle would be fought by the carrier aircraft.

On 3 and 4 May American aircraft spotted the Japanese invasion fleet. In the ensuing engagement aircraft from the *Yorktown* sank a Japanese destroyer and three minesweepers and damaged several other vessels. Fletcher was disappointed with the results;

it was the troop transports which he had hoped to eliminate. On 5 May he reunited the *Yorktown* and the *Lexington* and proceeded across the Coral Sea toward Port Moresby to link with Admiral Crace's cruisers. Intelligence reports received from island monitors informed Fletcher that the Japanese carrier force continued to approach Port Moresby. Although Fletcher had the advantage of knowing the general location of his enemy he did not have a fix on the exact position of the enemy carriers. The Japanese had no idea whatsoever that the American fleet was in the area as they believed the air strikes had originated from Port Moresby. However on 7 May Japanese reconnaissance aircraft sighted two American vessels, a tanker and a destroyer. They reported that they had seen a cruiser and a carrier and the Japanese commander launched a full air attack against the vessels. The destroyer was sunk but the tanker limped on for four more days. The Japanese carrier commander was furious at having launched his force, and possibly betrayed his position, for such a meager objective. If the true American fleet had discovered his position during the raid, the Japanese carriers would certainly have been destroyed. In fact the American fleet had at that same time located the Japanese invasion force and the carrier *Shoho*. American aircraft intercepted the fleet north of the Louisiades and there sank the *Shoho*. The remaining Japanese vessels were damaged and disorganized. Without the carrier escort to protect them they turned and withdrew. The American pilots were ecstatic about their success. Not only had

Above: A lifeboat with survivors from the carrier *Lexington* after the Coral Sea battle.
Top right: An American destroyer moves in to rescue survivors from the burning *Lexington*.
Top left: Dauntless dive bombers aboard a US carrier early in the war. The Dauntless played a leading role in the Battle of the Coral Sea.
Right: Rear-Admiral Frank J Fletcher led the US forces at the Coral Sea.

they 'scratched one flat-top' from the Imperial Navy as a famous signal put it, they had provided the United States with its first true victory.

However the Battle of the Coral Sea was far from over. Admiral Fletcher altered course to find the Japanese carriers and a game of hide and seek began. In the early daylight hours of 8 May both Japanese and American reconnaissance planes located the opposing fleets. The carrier aircraft were launched and a full and bitter battle began. When it ended the Japanese carrier *Shokaku* was severely damaged and 43 Japanese aircraft shot down. The American fleet did not escape unscathed. Thirty-three American aircraft were lost and both carriers were damaged. The *Lexington* limped on but internal explosions wracked the ship until at 2200 on 8 May she was abandoned and sank. The *Yorktown* returned to Pearl Harbor under the skillful control of Admiral Fletcher, where she was repaired and refitted in record time for active duty in the next major confrontation in the Pacific.

Admiral Fletcher had achieved a great victory. The *Lexington*, a front line carrier, had been lost but the fleet had surpassed all expectations. One Japanese carrier had been sunk and another put out of action but most importantly the Japanese advance, if only a small portion of it, had at last been stopped. A toll had been taken of experienced Japanese pilots and aircraft which would prove devastating to the Japanese war machine as the war continued. The Battle of the Coral Sea was by no means a turning point, but it did prove that the Japanese were not invincible.

3 THE TIDE TURNS

Even as the American-Australian and Japanese fleets approached a confrontation in the Coral Sea, Yamamoto was issuing orders on 5 May for a two pronged offensive against the United States in the central and northern Pacific. The primary strategic objectives there were Midway and the Aleutian Islands. In Japanese hands, Midway would be an ideal location for an advance warning and reconnaissance base. It would also serve as a base from which to harass the Hawaiian Islands with bombing raids to disrupt American activity, or in support of a major Japanese offensive in the central Pacific. The capture of the Aleutian Islands would serve several purposes. Possession of those islands by either Japan or the United States offered distinct advantages and disadvantages to both. The three main islands, Kiska, Adak and Attu, were large enough to support both air and naval installations. Although their northerly position made them inhospitable, their strategic value was evident in their proximity to both Tokyo and the North American mainland. Just as the Japanese could use the islands as a base the inverse was also true and American possession and use of the islands could be a dangerous threat to the Japanese homeland. Most Japanese, who were not privileged to factual information about the Doolittle Raid on Tokyo, believed that the American 'secret base' was in the Aleutians and supported the efforts to take the area.

Above all Yamamoto saw an offensive against the Aleutians as a means to bait the US Pacific Fleet into moving into the north Pacific, or at least into dividing its strength, thus allowing the Japanese to destroy it piecemeal and take the more important Midway base. To accomplish this strategy the Japanese used approximately 200 ships, including no less than 11 battleships, 22 cruisers, 65 destroyers, 21 submarines and 8 carriers in the two sections of the operation. More than 600 aircraft, 400 of which were borne by the carriers alone, accompanied the fleet. The submarines were to play an important role patrolling the three primary corridors through which Yamamoto believed the American vessels would have to move to reach either the Aleutians or Midway. What Yamamoto did not realize was that the American fleet, including the carriers, was already in the area of Midway and would never be contacted by the patrolling sub-

marines. There were further disadvantages to the Japanese. The lack of current, precise intelligence led the Japanese command to believe that there were only two American carriers, the USS *Enterprise* and the USS *Hornet*, in position in the central Pacific. It was not known that the *Yorktown* had been repaired and was fully battle-ready for the impending engagement.

As the Japanese fleet initiated the two pronged strategy, the 12 transports, four heavy cruisers and the destroyer escort vessels which made up the Midway fleet moved into position. Also in support of that invasion force were two battleships, four more heavy cruisers, a number of destroyers and one light carrier for direct air support. Behind the invasion fleet was the First Carrier Fleet of four front-line aircraft carriers, the *Akagi, Kaga, Hiryu* and *Soryu*, which were escorted by two battleships as well as heavy cruisers and yet more destroyers. The carrier air-

craft were to overcome the Midway defenses. Finally Yamamoto himself was with the reserve fleet of three battleships, two heavy cruisers and escort destroyers. The Aleutian invasion fleet was vastly different, being comprised of three transports carrying 2400 men plus two heavy cruisers with destroyer escorts. Some distance behind were two light carriers with an escort of destroyers and older battleships.

The plan was that the Aleutian Islands would be invaded first to draw the American ships from the central Pacific. Once the Japanese had accomplished this they would invade Midway, capture it, then set their main battle fleet to destroy the American fleet once and for all. However, the Americans had the enormous advantage of having broken the Japanese code. Intercepted Japanese transmissions indicated that there was to be a secondary attack in the Aleutians and a primary invasion elsewhere, but the Ameri-

Above: A rare moment of relaxation for the crew of the US *Fletcher* Class destroyer *O'Bannon.*
Top: Torpedo tube maintenance aboard the *O'Bannon.*
Right: A Douglas Dauntless dive bomber comes in to land on a US carrier, probably the *Ranger.*

cans could not break the codeword which gave the location. It was assumed that Midway was the most likely target. To confirm the site the American command transmitted an open message that a water purification plant on Midway had malfunctioned. The Intelligence sources then listened carefully for Japanese comment and when the Japanese response was intercepted the code name used matched that previously used for the Japanese invasion target. The American commander at Pearl Harbor, Admiral Nimitz, now knew where the battle was to be, he had only to decide how best to fight it.

Nimitz was not prepared to let Midway, the westernmost island of the Hawaiian chain, fall into Japanese hands and whether or not he thought the American fleet was ready for the challenge, the Japanese threat must be met. By conventional standards the American fleet had been severely handicapped by the raid on Pearl Harbor. On paper the fleet was no match for the Japanese. Yamamoto had eight carriers and 11 battleships supporting the two invasions while the United States had no battleships and only three carriers with which to respond. The Aleutian attack was begun on 27 May and before 2–3 June when the Japanese approach to Midway was to take place Nimitz ordered his carriers stationed where the Japanese would least expect them, north and east of the path of the main Japanese strike force. Thus the

Japanese, having no accurate information on the American fleet, proceeded as scheduled with all four of the primary carriers launching attacks against Midway early on 4 June.

When these attacks had been carried out the Japanese command decided that since reconnaissance aircraft had not seen the American carriers in the area, a second wave of attacks would be launched against Midway rather than holding aircraft to defend against or attack American vessels. However, American reconnaissance aircraft had located the Japanese fleet and all three American carriers launched full attacks with some 300 aircraft. The initial wave of American torpedo planes had little success against the Japanese defenses, scoring no satisfactory hits while having their own ranks decimated by the anti-aircraft power of the Japanese vessels. The second wave of the American attack included dive bombers from the *Enterprise*. With amazing accuracy the American planes sank the *Kaga* and the *Akagi* almost immediately. The dive bomber group from *Yorktown* was almost as successful, disabling the *Soryu* and damaging the *Hiryu*. The *Soryu* sank after the attack but the crew of the *Hiryu* succeeded in launching its aircraft in pursuit of the Americans. Following the American aircraft back to their carriers undetected, the Japanese caught the American fleet off guard. The *Yorktown* was struck and unlike the recent escape in the Coral Sea, was sunk. But this was the extent of the Japanese success. American aircraft from the *Hornet* and *Enterprise* returned to the Japanese fleet and in a devastating attack destroyed the last of Yamamoto's large carriers.

His carriers gone, Yamamoto saw no point in pursuing the invasion attempt. Nimitz's forces had scored a magnificent victory with four Japanese carriers sunk for the loss of only one American carrier. The invasion was repulsed and Midway saved. Perhaps most importantly the Japanese defeat had cost not only the invaluable carriers but at least 250 veteran Japanese aircrew who could not be replaced. Although the Japanese pressed on with their attacks in the South Pacific and the Aleutian Islands, the Battle of Midway proved that Japan's domination of the seas had been as brief as it was awesome. What the United States now needed, after the Coral Sea and Midway engagements, was a victory on land to announce a complete reversal of the unimpeded Japanese acquisition of Pacific territories. That land battle would occur on a rather out of the way island in the Solomons, Guadalcanal.

The Japanese were strengthening their position in the southern Pacific and in spite of the setbacks at sea decided that they must consolidate their power over the area. They decided to take and fortify the Solomons and New Guinea. As the naval invasion of Port Moresby had been repulsed during the Coral Sea

Above: Marine raiders leave an attack transport early in the Guadalcanal operation.
Top right: A Grumman Avenger of the Midway defense force.
Left: Home comforts in a Guadalcanal foxhole.

Battle, the Japanese decided to take the port by land, attacking from the northern coast across the central mountain range. The complete capture of the Solomons was to be the second phase of this operation and Guadalcanal was to be the site of a Japanese airbase. A base there and one at Port Moresby would enable the Japanese effectively to sever the lines of communication and cooperation between the United States and Australia and would for the most part give Japan supremacy over the entire south Pacific. Midway, and to a lesser extent the Battle of Coral Sea, dramatized the vulnerability of the carriers. The reliance of the forces in the Pacific on the airplane made it imperative that a more secure method for their deployment be found. The prevailing theory therefore became that while carriers could be sunk, islands could not, and although airfields could be temporarily incapacitated by the enemy, they could likewise be restored. Thus the Japanese and the United States and its allies began to look toward establishing island airfields in the best possible locations for their future needs.

Together MacArthur and Nimitz decided that in

the wake of two American naval victories the time had come for the United States to take a more offensive role. With the pressure off the Hawaiian Islands, American naval forces set course for the Solomons and the southwest Pacific. Originally the American command planned a three phase seizure of the area but when it was learned that the Japanese were building an airfield on Guadalcanal the United States shifted attention to that island and the airfield at Lunga Point. Guadalcanal was an island with dimensions of approximately 90 by 125 miles. The terrain included steep mountains, thick grasslands and rain forests and swamps that provided excellent habitat for the malaria-carrying anopheles mosquito. Only the northern portion of the island was in the least hospitable and it was there that airfield construction had begun. The initial American force assembled for the assault contained three aircraft carriers, the *Wasp*, *Saratoga* and the *Enterprise*, all under the tactical command of Admiral Fletcher. The landing fleet was commanded by Rear-Admiral Kelly Turner and was comprised of a mixed force of American and Australian cruisers and destroyers. The Australian naval commander present was Rear-Admiral Victor Crutchley, Royal Navy. The Marine landing force consisted of 19,000 troops from the 1st Marine Division and one regiment of the 2nd Marine Division, Brigadier General Alexander Vandegrift commanding. Land-based aircraft from Fiji, New Caledonia and the New Hebrides were also to support the invasion.

The landing was to be accomplished in two parts. The first and more important was against Guadalcanal itself while the second was against the smaller island of Tulagi. On 26 July 1942 the Allied invasion fleet and its escorts set out for their destination. By 7 August Guadalcanal was in sight. The Japanese were taken by surprise as the American vessels appeared. Their reconnaissance aircraft had spotted the American vessels only late on the previous day and there had been little time to prepare an adequate defense. American naval vessels and aircraft began the assault with a heavy bombardment of the island and at 0900 hours the Marines went ashore. The

opposition met was minimal and by evening 11,000 Marines had landed. They captured the airfield, which was almost completed and had suffered little damage in the initial bombardment, and eliminated a Japanese force of more than 2000, most of whom were construction workers, not soldiers. It had been thought that Guadalcanal would present a difficult objective but in fact Tulagi was harder to take. It was not until the following day that a force of approximately 6000 Marines was able to overcome the resistance of the 1600 Japanese troops. Although the fighting on Tulagi was fierce, it was a mere skirmish when compared to what lay ahead in the Pacific. Although the Japanese troops fought to the bitter end, in two days the Americans had thrown the Imperial Command off balance. It had been only eight months to the day since the Japanese had allegedly dealt the United States a death blow at Pearl Harbor, yet the Americans had begun a successful counteroffensive securing one of Japan's most distant yet 'high priority' perimeter bases.

With the loss of Guadalcanal and Tulagi the Japanese effort in the southwest Pacific region was in chaos. Activation of the airfield would allow American aircraft to strike at key Japanese installations, the most important of which was Rabaul on New Britain in the Bismarck Archipelago. At first the Japanese made sporadic counterattacks against the support fleet and the Guadalcanal airfield, now known as

Henderson Field, but little damage was inflicted as the Americans were given fair warning by Australian coast watchers who monitored any activity of Japanese vessels and aircraft. However, within 48 hours of the invasion, the Japanese had hastily prepared a force of heavy and light cruisers and one destroyer. They planned to attack at night, bringing enough firepower to bear against the American fleet to force it to withdraw from the area. Although the Japanese fleet was spotted as it left Rabaul it slipped undetected through the Slot (the body of water between the twin chins of the Solomons). En route it acquired the support of two seaplane carriers. As the Japanese fleet approached, the American carriers withdrew from the invasion force, leaving only the vessels of Admirals Turner and Crutchley to protect the landing force. As the Allied ships waited off Savo Island, their destroyers patrolled the waters in search of the Japanese fleet which they believed was approaching.

At 0130 hours on 9 August the Japanese vessels passed through the outer American perimeter to engage the American and Australian invasion fleet. The action was swift and decisive. The Allies had spent little time working in tandem and were overwhelmed. By 0215 hours the Japanese fleet was withdrawing, while off Guadalcanal Allied cruisers and destroyers were either foundering or burning. The Japanese vessels were untouched but, believing that American carriers were nearby, they retired rapidly toward

Above: The five Sullivan brothers seen at the commissioning ceremony of the light cruiser *Juneau* (CL.52) in February 1942. All five were killed during the naval Battle of Guadalcanal in November when the *Juneau* was sunk. An American destroyer was later named *The Sullivans* to commemorate the family's sacrifice.
Left: The antiaircraft defenses of the carrier *Enterprise* which served in all the major actions during the Guadalcanal campaign and soldiered on until the end of the Pacific war.
Far left: Crewmen load a 500-pound bomb on a Dauntless aboard the *Enterprise* off Guadalcanal on 7 August 1942.

Rabaul before daylight could expose them to attack. Had the Japanese commander realized that the carriers were no longer in the vicinity and pressed his attack, the remaining troop transports and supply ships would certainly have been destroyed, thus isolating the Americans on the islands and ending the invasion operation.

The American command was in a state of panic. Four cruisers and more than 1000 men had been lost. Another 1000 Marines and a large part of the supplies for the whole force had yet to be taken ashore. A five-mile defensive perimeter was established on Guadalcanal as the Americans waited for a Japanese counter-offensive. However the Japanese were unaware of the dangerously precarious American situation and were focussing attention on their own land invasion to capture Port Moresby. It was not until 17 August that six Japanese destroyers landed more than 1000 Japanese troops under the command of Colonel Ichiki on Guadalcanal. Their objective was to recapture Henderson Field and destroy the American aircraft stationed there. By the night of 20 August the Japanese were prepared for their attack but by then the American Marines had been given adequate time to recover from the shock of the naval engagement. Ichiki's forces were literally eliminated to a man before ever reaching the airfield.

During that same period the Japanese were laying a trap for the American carriers. A light carrier, cruiser and two destroyers were sent through the Slot to attract American attention. Once this was done the Japanese carriers *Zuikaku* and *Shokaku* would send their aircraft against the Americans, to be followed by an attack from a third Japanese fleet of two battleships and three heavy cruisers. Admiral Fletcher and his carriers had returned to the Solomons and on 24 August the bait was spotted. Sixty-seven bombers were launched to intercept the Japanese light carrier, which was promptly destroyed. The *Zuikaku* and *Shokaku* then sent their attack forces against Fletcher's fleet, but the Americans were prepared. Fletcher had kept his fighter aircraft with the carriers for just such an event. He also had the additional support of the new American battleship *North Carolina* and her escorts. The combination of American fighter aircraft and antiaircraft fire took its toll. Eighty of the 90 Japanese aircraft were destroyed. The *Saratoga* launched a second wave of aircraft which severely damaged one of the Japanese seaplane carriers.

Though Fletcher had lost only 17 aircraft in the exchange he maneuvered his fleet from the area. The Japanese carriers had not suffered damage but had lost their offensive air capability, which forced them to withdraw. The Japanese surface fleet pushed on through the Slot to locate the American carriers, which they believed had been seriously damaged in the air attack. However, this error was discovered before they closed in with the American carriers and the fleet ceased pursuit. Once again a battle had been fought without either fleet gaining a marked advantage in terms of ships sunk but as before the Japanese had suffered devastating aircrew losses.

On 25 August the Japanese continued to try to push ships and troops through the Slot. On this occasion American aircraft from Henderson Field drove the fleet back, damaging one cruiser and sinking a troop transport. The second round of naval duels had slightly favored the Americans but the Japanese continued successfully to harass American operations. On 31 August the carrier *Saratoga* was struck by a torpedo and forced out of action for repairs for three months. Two weeks later the *Wasp* was sunk and the battleship *North Carolina* was damaged while escorting a convoy to the Solomons. The American situation was quite grim especially after the *Hornet* was sunk in the Battle of Santa Cruz in October leaving the damaged *Enterprise* as the only US carrier operational in the Pacific. The American tactic became one of landing troops and supplies in daylight with air cover from Henderson Field, while withdrawing to the open sea at night to hide from the Japanese destroyers patrolling the Solomon waters.

In early September the Japanese succeeded in

Above: Japanese naval troops operating a heavy machine gun. The original of this picture was taken from a prisoner on Guadalcanal.
Right: The listing flight deck of the carrier *Enterprise* during the Battle of Santa Cruz. A Wildcat fighter is being manhandled.
Below right: A typical Guadalcanal scene after a Japanese attack.
Below: A group of Marines pauses for a break before moving further into the Guadalcanal jungle. This picture was taken in August 1942.

landing 6000 troops on Guadalcanal via the 'Tokyo Express,' a system of shuttles made by Japanese destroyers and troop transports. On 13 and 14 September those troops attacked American Marines at a point known as Bloody Ridge. The Marines suffered heavy casualties but the Japanese force was destroyed. In November a Japanese convoy carrying approximately 10,000 men was intercepted by American forces. Several Japanese vessels which were not destroyed were beached, allowing some 4000 troops to go ashore. Sporadic action at Guadalcanal continued until February 1943, by which time the Americans had overcome the Japanese threat and begun to take full control of the Solomon Islands. For the Japanese the prolonged battle for Guadalcanal was devastating. They sacrificed 25,000 men to American losses of just over 1600. Although both sides lost approximately equal numbers of ships, the loss of life in the Japanese fleet will never be known but is estimated much higher than American and Allied losses. The Japanese were also deprived of at least 900 trained aircrew. The United States lost a minute fraction of that number and more importantly was daily gaining experience as Japan was losing it. The United States was now prepared to begin to roll back the tide of Japanese expansion throughout the Pacific.

4 PACIFIC SIDESHOWS

There were two principal sideshow arenas in the Pacific for the United States – China and the Aleutian Islands. Although both were considered important targets for the ultimate defeat of Japan, neither had the crucial priority that MacArthur and Halsey had in the South Pacific or Nimitz in the Central Pacific.

China, for all its centuries of civilization, was viewed as the awkward child of the Pacific. It had been at war with Japan since the 1930s. Manchuria was the primary issue but the Imperial Command saw all of China as a vast manpower and resource pool and a ready market in the Japanese economic sphere. Japan also viewed China with a colonialistic perspective; it was a possession to be gained rather than an independent sovereign state. America had been involved in China for many years. During the colonial era as European powers extended their grip around the world, with China no exception to their expansion, the United States displayed an unusual kinship toward China. On more than one occasion the United States aided China against the Europeans and their colonial aspirations in the Far East. The United States took pride in this relationship, trading with China while keeping unwarranted interference in Chinese affairs to a minimum. There were naturally disagreements but the atmosphere remained relatively friendly throughout.

In the 1930s the Manchurian Incident between Japan and China triggered an angry response from the United States, which informed the Japanese government that it did not recognize Japan's sovereignty over this or any other area Japan might take by force. The Japanese government ignored the United States, as it also ignored the League of Nations, but the incident reaffirmed a growing rift between the United States and Japan and solidified the bond with China. From January 1932 when the United States issued this statement of policy to Japan, America became increasingly wary of Japanese activity in the Pacific and Far East. As the United States held possessions in the Pacific, including the Philippines, Guam and Wake Island, the potential of Japan as a future foe had to be acknowledged.

Throughout the 1930s Japan maintained its pressure in China and in 1936 declared itself the master race in the Far East. The claim was strikingly similar to that made by Nazi Germany and although separated by distance and culture the ultimate objectives of each were clear. In 1937 Japanese forces invaded China proper and for several years held the upper hand. However, China was too vast, swallowing up the Japanese armies, until Japan was forced to be content to hold the coastal regions and main strategic areas. During those years not only the United States but also Britain and the USSR, with whom the Japanese had border clashes, began to send supplies and materiel to bolster the Chinese resistance forces.

By October 1940 China was prepared to ask for even more assistance. Chiang Kai-shek approached President Roosevelt on the issue of sending aircraft to China for use against Japan. He initially requested 500 aircraft of all types, including heavy bombers and fighters and the pilots and crews with which to man that air force. Although the United States was at odds with Japan, FDR realized that such blatant interference could propel the two countries into a war for which the United States was not prepared. Roosevelt saw Nazi Germany as the most formidable threat to American security and was certain that the two nations would soon be brought to grips. However, the American President was finally persuaded to consider Chiang Kai-shek's proposal. But 500 aircraft and crews was an impossible order. A compromise was struck. China would receive a greatly reduced number of aircraft but they would include the front-line P-40B Tomahawk fighter. This model was in many ways inferior to the fighter aircraft of other nations but it was one of the strongest aircraft of its time. It was able to tolerate a great deal of abuse in handling and from enemy fire and was second to none in ground-attack capabilities.

The Tomahawk's legend would be made in China with a group of American volunteers known as the Flying Tigers. They were commanded by one of the United States' most brilliant pilots, the then recently retired Colonel Claire Chennault. Chennault was asked not only to command the American Volunteer Group but also to take control of the Chinese Air Force. With some 100 Tomahawks and pilots who were released from service obligations in the US Army and Navy, Chennault formed the nucleus of the Chinese Air Force. In November 1941 the American

Volunteer Group (AVG) met in Burma where they received their aircraft, which had been sent to China under the Lend-Lease arrangements. From that point on their exploits would become magnified, held up to the world and the US Air Corps as an example to be emulated. The Flying Tigers were financed by the United States via China and their incentives included a $500 bonus for each enemy aircraft shot down. By the time the war ended the Flying Tigers unit had been expanded to become the Tenth Air Force.

By the outbreak of war between Japan and the United States in December 1941, 40 of the 51 Japanese Army divisions were tied in China, their efforts divided between Chiang Kai-shek's Nationalist Army in the south and the Communist forces in the north. The Nationalist forces were located in the south primarily because their lifeline to American and British supplies, the Burma Road, ran through that region. Shortly after war was declared the United States sent General Stilwell to China as military adviser to Chiang Kai-shek to ensure that military aid to the Nationalist Army was properly directed and applied. His other purpose was to urge the Chinese to increase pressure on the Japanese so that Japanese divisions would be immobilized in China, unable to be siphoned off for use in the Pacific. Stilwell was critical of the Chinese and often found himself the center of controversy between the United States and Chinese governments. Although he was doing an excellent job of reorganizing the Chinese army and successfully trained and equipped three divisions in India, he found it impossible to convince the Nationalists to mount a major offensive against the Japanese except in and near Burma. This situation would continue throughout the war.

The other action in which American forces participated on the continent was in Burma. In early 1943

Above: A B-29 Superfortress bomber of 14th Air Force at a base in China. The operations of the 14th Air Force provoked major Japanese offensives against its bases in 1944 and 1945.
Right: Major General Chennault, Commanding General of the 14th Air Force. Chennault came into conflict with Stilwell and Chiang Kai-shek over the allocation of supplies sent to China.

long-range penetration groups were formed under the command of British Brigadier General Orde Wingate. His concepts of jungle warfare and theories of movement and resupply from the air revolutionized these aspects of military procedure. An American volunteer force, the 5307th Provisional Regiment commanded by Brigadier General Frank Merrill undertook similar operations. Merrill's Marauders would become as well known as the Flying Tigers, their aviator counterparts. They proved that American soldiers were more than a match for the Japanese and that they could survive as well in the jungles as their Asian counterparts. After successfully engaging the Japanese in the Hukawng and Mogaung Valleys in northern Burma and assisting in the capture of Myitkyina, Merrill's Marauders were deactivated on 10 August 1944. Although there were other US units in China and Burma American efforts on the Asian continent were primarily in the air helping supply the Chinese armies. It was the British, whose interests in India and China were strongest, who would be most deeply involved.

During the period of stalemate after the Battle of Midway and before the United States could generate and deploy its forces for the counteroffensive in the Pacific, the issue concerning the Aleutian Islands arose. This particular sideshow was dubbed 'The Thousand Mile War' as that was roughly the distance from the American bases on Alaska's coast to the most westerly island of the Aleutian chain.

The Aleutians were perhaps the least hospitable of the islands in the Pacific. Contrary to stereotype, they were not covered with jungles or malaria swamps, but they did offer unique disadvantages. They lay in an area where fog, rain and snow dominated. At certain times of the year it rained so steadily and the ground became so saturated that it was virtually impossible to walk, let alone launch or land aircraft. More aircraft were lost in the Aleutians due to fog and airfield conditions than due to enemy fire or attack. The weather in the summer months could also reach a hot, humid extreme which bred swarms of insects and from which there was no relief of shade on the tundra-like landscapes. In the winter months when there were few hours of daylight the temperature dropped so low that a man could freeze in a matter of minutes. While little attention was focussed on the Aleutians, service duty there was at least as, if not more, unpleasant than throughout the rest of the Pacific.

Although both the United States and Japan recognized the inherent difficulties, control of the two primary islands of Kiska and Attu provided sufficient strategic advantage to make the effort worthwhile. When the news of a Japanese invasion of the islands during the Midway offensive reached the United States, panic was sparked on the West Coast. The proximity of the enemy and his supposed ability to strike as far south as San Francisco forced the United States to react quickly. American aircraft stationed in Alaska began bombing raids against Kiska and Attu to be accompanied by naval bombardments in the months ahead. By 30 August 1942 American troops had taken the island of Adak, 200 miles east of Kiska. Airfield construction on Adak was begun immediately to assist in the recapture of Kiska and Attu. It was not until January 1943, however, that American forces finally captured Amchitka Island, 90 miles east of Kiska. One month later, plans were set in motion for the capture of Attu, the weaker Japanese island position. In mid-March a naval squadron commanded by Rear-Admiral Alexander McMorris formed a blockade around Attu with two cruisers and four destroyers. On 26 March the blockade intercepted a Japanese force bound for Attu. The Japanese had a distinct advantage but in the ensuing battle McMorris' vessels forced them to withdraw.

On 11 May 11,000 American troops of the 7th Infantry Division were landed on Attu. For two more weeks the Japanese garrison of 2000 troops held out, being steadily driven from the shores to the mountainous inland region. The Japanese position was critical and on 29 May they counterattacked. For almost 24 hours the Japanese mounted suicidal attacks against

overwhelming odds. The battle finally ended when only 28 Japanese soldiers remained. The Americans had sustained 600 casualties but the victory bolstered American morale and gave new impetus to the island-hopping scheme of airbases on one island supporting the landings on another. It was in fact such support, along with naval assistance, which kept the American casualties low during the Japanese counterattacks.

The Japanese-held island of Kiska had now been virtually surrounded. Seaplane reconnaissance informed the Japanese command of the gravity of the situation. Reinforcements would be needed if they hoped to break the encirclement or defend the island. However, by the summer of 1943 Japanese operations in the southwest Pacific were too important to permit troop or ship relocations to the Aleutians. The decision was made to give up Kiska. On 28 July a fleet of Japanese cruisers and destroyers approached the island under cover of fog. In less than one hour they removed the entire Kiska garrison without detection. Completely unaware of the withdrawal, American air and naval forces continued to bombard the island. After more than two weeks of this activity, an invasion force of 34,000 American and Canadian troops landed on 15 August. For the next five days these troops advanced cautiously across the island. They could not determine the tactics the Japanese were employing. Tension mounted as the hours and days passed and casualties were taken as nervous units accidentally fired on their own troops. Finally embarrassed American commanders declared the island secure.

The Aleutian campaign, which utilized the combined strengths of more than 100,000 American and Canadian troops, a large naval task force of battleships, cruisers and destroyers and the 11th Army Air Corps was over. Had the American command made better use of its intelligence concerning the Japanese threat to the American and Canadian coastlines, the majority of these troops and their support could have been more effectively deployed elsewhere in the Pacific. As it was the Japanese invasion of the Aleutians was partially successful, drawing off a large Allied force from the central and southern Pacific operations.

In their respective manners each of these Pacific sideshows had an effect on the American position in the war with Japan. They served as proving grounds for American tactics and as morale boosters for the troops and the American people. Both were essential in the grim and bitter fighting which would at times dishearten the United States in its island efforts.

Left: Chennault chats with members of his staff and a group of 14th Air Force pilots in front of a fighter plane.
Below left: 'Vinegar Joe' Stilwell enjoys his 1943 Christmas dinner.
Right: The control tower of Myitkyina airfield, Burma.
Below: Admiral Kinkaid commanded the Aleutians operations.

5 NEW GUINEA AND THE SOLOMONS

As the battle of Guadalcanal continued, the United States was gaining confidence in its ability to defeat the Japanese, though it was quite clear that the struggle for the ultimate defeat of Japan would be bitter and costly. Although the Japanese had achieved great victories more quickly than was believed possible, the United States was proving that those victories had not been as complete as was first imagined. The United States was now locked in combat not only in the Pacific but in Europe and the intensity of American mobilization toward the European Front would have a marked effect on the approach taken to accomplish total victory in the Pacific. The five fronts in the Pacific made it imperative that the United States carefully consider the direction and objectives which would provide the most expedient road to that victory.

Both President Roosevelt and Prime Minister Winston Churchill viewed the Pacific issues as secondary to the war effort against Nazi Germany. Once Germany was defeated Churchill was willing to direct all Allied attention against Japan. Until then he refused to give consideration to plans giving priority to the Pacific Theater. Churchill often strongly voiced his opinions on the American Pacific endeavor, stating that it detracted from American operations which might have been conducted in Europe. Although British forces operated in Asia, their role was primarily one of extended defense to keep the Japanese from making further conquests until European issues were settled. This policy, that the Pacific war was somehow not as important as that which raged in Europe, was not acceptable to all American military leaders. The most outspoken of these was General Douglas MacArthur. He saw the Pacific Theater as the real war and the European conflict as something which the United States had unwisely been dragged into. MacArthur's opinion must of course be tempered with the knowledge that he had spent many years in the Pacific and was obsessed with the recapture of the Philippines. It was nevertheless an argument which had some justification.

In May 1943 the Allies discussed their plans at the Trident Conference held in Washington, DC. The long range plans for breaching the Japanese island perimeter and the Allied counteroffensive were presented. The issues were fundamentally the same as

had been discussed at the Casablanca Conference in January 1943 but Trident was a more modest approach. The central Pacific operations had yet to be formally proposed. To fill the void in that area and to establish a working strategy, the American government sent Admiral King to the Pacific. Although there was an idea of the intended direction, there were problems and varying viewpoints on the execution of a strategy to be resolved. The main idea for the Pacific advance being to move forward quickly it was suggested that the plan should be to take only those

Left: Vice-Admiral William F Halsey replaced Admiral Ghormley as Commander of the South Pacific Area in October 1942.
Far left: MacArthur (right) with General Sir Thomas Blamey the Australian officer who led the Allied land forces in the New Guinea campaign.
Below: The heavy cruisers *Chicago* and *Louisville* seen in January 1943 shortly before the *Chicago* was sunk while escorting a supply convoy to Guadalcanal.

islands that had strategic importance – as was being done in Operation Cartwheel in the Solomons. This was contrary to the conventional military strategy of moving forward en masse to capture an entire given area. It was based on the belief that once the primary islands had fallen the others would be isolated and thus ineffective.

Again MacArthur was opposed to the theory being applied. The island-hopping strategy was to be applied primarily in Nimitz's Central Pacific Area. Large numbers of men, ships, aircraft and supplies would be tied to these operations. MacArthur thought they would serve a more fruitful purpose elsewhere, as in the Philippines for example. He argued further that amphibious operations to take fortified atolls would prove more costly in lives than was justified by the accomplishments. Perhaps most importantly, MacArthur considered an offensive in the central Pacific to be a waste of time. He argued that an American offensive through New Guinea to the Philippines offered a better path toward Japan as land-based aircraft could support the operation along the way. The central Pacific strategy required large fleets of carriers and their escorts to pursue and support land invasions. There was therefore an increased risk of Japanese victory on the open sea, which could have a serious effect on the entire war effort. MacArthur received support from Britain on this issue as Churchill thought more American naval power should be directed toward the Atlantic.

Finally the strategy for the primary fronts, with the Central Pacific and the Southwest Pacific being most important, was agreed. Smaller operations were to be maintained in the North Pacific around the Aleutians, and in the South Pacific from the Solomon Islands. Five commands were established. Admiral Nimitz commanded the Central Pacific Area and the northern Pacific operations. In the South Pacific Admiral WF 'Bull' Halsey commanded the operations to strike from the New Hebrides through the Solomons with the New Britain port of Rabaul and the Bismarck Archipelago as his ultimate objectives. The Southwest Pacific Area was commanded by General MacArthur whose goal was to drive from Australia through New Guinea to support Halsey's operations in the Solomons, then to continue on to recapture the Philippines. The final command was on the Asian continent where British Admiral Lord Mountbatten, supported by General Stilwell's command, would continue to operate in India, Burma and Southeast Asia. The intended advances were to continue in full swing until the end of 1944, at which time the situation would be reviewed with the objective of reaching the final stages of an offensive against the Japanese Home Islands.

The tactical details of these operations had now to be resolved. The most experienced troops in the area were MacArthur's 1st and 2nd Marine Divisions.

They were shifted from his command to the Central Pacific command. The inexperienced 27th Infantry Division, which had just finished its training in Hawaii, replaced the Marines in MacArthur's forces. In so doing the precedent was set that though the Army would have its role and particular function in the strategic plans, it would be the Marines who led the Central Pacific operations.

By the end of February 1943, Guadalcanal and nearby Russell Island were secured with the added weight of the 43rd Infantry Division. Although both the Americans and Japanese had suffered aircraft and ship losses, Japanese troop losses were 12 times as great. Guadalcanal had become the site of both air and naval bases which would be essential to support the drive through the Solomons. The victory there was matched by MacArthur's efforts in New Guinea. The Japanese had taken the northern coastal area around Buna in July 1942 and had consolidated their forces before striking across the central mountains and jungles in their bid to take Port Moresby by land. More than 11,000 Japanese troops surprised the Allied forces in New Guinea by crossing what had been considered impassable terrain. However, the Japanese lacked sufficient air support for their offensive and the air superiority of MacArthur's American and Australian command proved to be the deciding factor. By late September 1942 MacArthur's troops had begun to push the Japanese back. The Japanese troops fought fiercely but within one month they were forced back to Buna. The port was besieged and in January 1943 Japanese resistance collapsed and Buna fell.

With the victory in New Guinea secured, MacArthur and Halsey began to look toward their primary objective, Rabaul, the strongest Japanese base in the area. Both commanders knew the critical importance of Rabaul as the source of Japanese influence in the region. Much had to be done before the base could be eliminated. Even by combining forces MacArthur and Halsey did not have the strength to take Rabaul in a direct assault. It was therefore decided that they would proceed to eliminate supporting Japanese bases in the Solomons and New Britain, wearing down the Japanese strength slowly. The strategy was sound but on this occasion fate played an important role in the Allied success.

In mid-April 1943 the commander of the Japanese Combined Fleet, Admiral Yamamoto, decided to visit the island of Bougainville. His mission was to bolster morale, while at the same time gaining first-hand information on the situation and determining the extent of Japanese needs in men and materiel. Naturally, coded messages informed the Japanese bases of the admiral's impending arrival. These transmissions were intercepted and relayed to Admiral Halsey. Not only did they reveal the arrival of the Japanese commander but they also told of the number of aircraft in his flight and the route he would be using. The information seemed too good to be true but the situation was hurriedly reviewed and it was decided to attempt to ambush Yamamoto. The American-educated Japanese commander was recognized as the driving intelligence behind Japanese operations and it was considered that the loss of his expertise could take months, even years, off the war in the Pacific. The Japanese would be seriously crippled by the loss of so important a military figure in morale alone.

On the morning of 18 April 1943, 18 P-38 fighter aircraft struck at the two Japanese bombers and their escorts. The P-38s had flown to their limits to make the interception but Admiral Yamamoto's well-known reputation for punctuality proved to be his undoing. At precisely the designated hour his flight appeared. The Japanese fighter escort was brushed aside and Yamamoto's aircraft crashed in flames. Captain TG Lanphier of the Army Air Corps was credited with the kill. Yamamoto's death would place the Japanese Imperial Command at a serious disadvantage in the impending American offensive.

By 30 June 1943 Halsey and MacArthur had begun to advance. Halsey landed troops on New Georgia while MacArthur moved to Nassau Bay, New Guinea. New Georgia fell and Halsey looked toward Bougainville. MacArthur, however, was intent on eliminating the Japanese from New Guinea completely. He prepared to capture Lae and Salamaua. His 9th Australian Division landed at Lae in September and more than 1500 paratroopers were dropped to cut off the Japanese retreat. By mid-September both Lae and Salamaua were taken and by the end of that month MacArthur had cleared this section of New Guinea of enemy troops. New Georgia was by that time also secured and within the next month Halsey's forces had taken Treasury Island and Choiseul.

With these objectives gained, Halsey was able to attack Bougainville on 1 November. The Japanese had every intention of halting the American advance, at least until the defense at Rabaul could be fortified. The 60,000 Japanese troops on Bougainville were concentrated on the southern half of the island, leaving the northern tip virtually undefended. Although landings were made, at first the battle for Bougainville was carried out chiefly in the air and at sea. Halsey sent his heavy bombers to pound the island. Almost immediately the Japanese responded with air and naval forces from Rabaul. Japanese aircraft suffered high casualties as American fighters drove them back. A Japanese cruiser and destroyer fleet arrived, bent on achieving a victory similar to that which had been gained during the initial American invasion of Guadalcanal. However, on this occasion the American fleet was prepared. Although the Japanese made repeated attacks, they were consistently repulsed with mounting casualties.

Above: Marine on the alert in the Bougainville jungle, November 1943.
Left: Unloading ammunition from landing craft at Rendova Island, New Georgia.
Below: Marines advance through the mud on Bougainville.

Halsey was convinced that the Japanese had sustained devastating losses and on 5 and 11 November he sent daring raids to Rabaul. American carrier aircraft struck the naval and air bases with such ferocity that the Japanese air force at Rabaul was almost completely destroyed and naval vessels were forced to flee to the open sea to escape destruction in port. By 12 November the Japanese fleet in the area was considered nonexistent. Halsey's 3rd Marine Division had gained a beachhead on Bougainville which they now enlarged with the help of the 37th Infantry Division. Later the Americal Division, which replaced the Marines, would join with the 37th Division to take full possession of Bougainville. The final Japanese assault did not occur until March 1944. From 8 to 20 March, the fighting was the fiercest seen on the island with 15,000 Japanese involved. None-

theless the island was secured and the Solomon Islands' campaign was over. Australian units were then called in to replace American troops who prepared to continue the advance.

MacArthur had by this time moved on also. As his Australian forces proceeded in New Guinea, US Marine units took Cape Gloucester on New Britain on 26 December 1943. They advanced through the island from that western point but Halsey's attacks had devastated the Japanese position at Rabaul, making it unnecessary to expend precious lives in a direct assault on that base. With Rabaul no longer a threat and Halsey established on Bougainville, MacArthur struck at the Admiralty Islands on 29 February 1944. This sealed the fate of Rabaul and provided MacArthur with a staging site for a spectacular return to the Philippines.

6 ACROSS THE CENTRAL PACIFIC

By the fall of 1943 the United States Navy was beginning to gain an advantage which was increasing daily. Although only roughly 20 months had passed since Pearl Harbor, the American shipbuilding industry had reacted quickly and was by this time producing whatever might be necessary to fight a war on two oceans. Both MacArthur and Halsey in the Southwest and South Pacific were driving toward their prospective objectives. Each island that fell meant more men, ships, aircraft and equipment could be spared from those fronts. It was then decided to proceed with the recapture of the Central Pacific perimeter island defenses. With the island-hopping strategy, the United States was prepared to take the war to the heart of Japan.

The concept continued to evoke controversy. It was alien to all military maxims to permit enemy forces to remain in the rear of a major advance. However, the information received in the initial offensives convinced Nimitz and King that the Japanese defensive perimeter was strong only if the United States chose to attack each fortified island. If the majority of islands was by-passed and only selected islands of primary strategic importance were taken, the Japanese perimeter would collapse. The fighting would be bloody, but the Japanese forces isolated on non-targeted islands by the strength of the patrolling US naval forces would be useless to the Japanese war effort. Captured islands were to be promptly converted into American air bases. The ultimate goal was to capture islands close enough to the main islands of Japan so that the newest American bomber, the B-29 Superfortress could strike at Japan itself. The argument finally boiled down to the simple truth that Nimitz favored the island-hopping scheme and until notice to the contrary he issued policy in the Pacific.

Fortunately this policy was producing results. The overextended Japanese forces were beginning to falter. They were far from beaten but the war's effects were being seen. The Japanese command had truly believed that the lightning advance, experienced leadership and the quality of the Japanese air and naval forces would take all hope of resistance from the United States and its allies. The Japanese had misjudged the nature and character of their enemies and such early responses as the Battle of the Coral Sea and

Midway had proved American determination. In the long term the industrial potential and manpower of the United States would surpass the initial Japanese advantage. The elite Japanese pilots and the Zero fighters had a heyday in 1941 and 1942. That reign was over by 1943 as the United States introduced durable aircraft and skilled air crews.

As the American strategy changed, so too did the naval forces on which so much depended. The battleship had traditionally been considered the ultimate factor on the seas. Even the Japanese, who revolutionized the strategic and tactical use of aircraft carriers, continued on the assumption that the mighty battleship was essential to the destruction of the enemy in sea battles. The United States of necessity turned its carriers into the primary vessels of the Pacific war. New battleships and cruisers were de-

signed which could keep pace with the carriers and which could act as floating antiaircraft batteries as well as surface combat support. The potential of the airplane was recognized and the carriers were the means of its deployment. This was the key.

The United States viewed the carrier as falling into two distinct classifications. Fleet carriers would become the backbone of the Navy and would have complements of 80–100 aircraft. These carriers would become the dominating forces in sea battles. The second classification was the escort carrier. These vessels were smaller and easier to build than the fleet carriers and were given the tasks of escorting transports and supply vessels on the open sea and supporting amphibious landings during the American island-hopping advance. This freed the fleet carriers to pursue their primary targets, Japanese vessels. Escort carriers also provided a ready reserve of aircraft to bring fleet carriers back to full strength after engagements, thus keeping the larger carriers fully operational.

The changes in naval tactics provoked yet another important innovation geared to maximize the effectiveness of the fleets. Traditionally fleets had set sail with primary objectives, accomplishing which exhausted the vessels' resources. They were then forced to return to friendly ports after each operation to refuel, resupply, rearm and repair before the next mission. The American command recognized this as a monumental waste of time and ships in an arena where both were of the essence to victory. Nimitz realized that island-hopping could only work if the American advance moved forward steadily, allowing the Japanese no opportunity to regain their balance. Also the idea of isolating and neutralizing Japanese-held islands could only be accomplished if the American fleets could maintain an active presence in the area. Japanese lines of supply and communication had to

Above: A Nakajima B5N 'Kate' torpedo bomber comes to grief while attacking an American carrier during an American strike on the Marshall Islands in 1943.
Top: One of the most famous Zeros of the war, a captured A6M5 Type O Carrier Fighter Model 52, seen here being tested by American experts.
Above left: Grumman Avengers and Douglas Dauntlesses of an American carrier group on the way to attack a Japanese island base early in 1944.
Right: Fighter pilots aboard the carrier Intrepid being briefed for a raid on Roi in the Marshall Islands, January 1944.

be blockaded. The issue was simple: combat vessels were useless if not in combat. The question to be answered: how could the United States keep its fleets permanently at sea? The answer was presented in the form of special service fleets. These resembled floating naval bases with supply and repair vessels, tankers, tenders, barges, tugs, hospital ships and floating dry docks. Virtually anything the combat fleets might require was to be found in the special service fleet. The carrier task forces, whose job it was to engage and destroy Japanese fleets; the amphibious assault forces, whose objectives were the island

Below: Marine throws a grenade at a Japanese position on Tarawa.
Left: Generals Holland Smith (left) and Julian C Smith inspect installations on Betio Atoll, Tarawa, after the battle.

fortresses; and the special service fleets, which kept the combat vessels battle-ready, were an invincible union of naval innovations. The United States was no longer tied to operations near friendly ports but could now advance to Japan, fighting all the way, free of the traditional restrictions that had long hampered naval operations.

This description was the foundation of the United States Fifth Fleet whose objective was to secure the Central Pacific. The overall commander of the Fifth Fleet was Vice-Admiral Raymond A Spruance, who was directly responsible to Admiral Nimitz at his Pearl Harbor headquarters. The fleet carriers were commanded by Rear-Admiral Charles A Pownall and the amphibious fleet by Rear-Admiral Turner. The Marines of the Fifth Fleet were commanded by Major General Holland 'Howling Mad' Smith. A land-based air contingent was also attached to the fleet. These aircraft were to provide support as island airfields were taken along the route. The Fifth Fleet's first assignment, given by Admiral King, was to take the Marshall Islands. However, Nimitz and his intelligence staff reviewed aerial reconnaissance photographs of the area and decided that a more gradual approach should be taken. He chose to test the Japanese strength and his fleet's new tactics on the Gilbert Islands first. Nimitz believed that an assault on the Gilberts would provide his fleet with amphibious landing experience against an easier target than the Marshalls. Once the invasion was complete, airfields established on the Tarawa and Makin Atolls of the Gilbert chain would provide increased air support for the Marshall Islands offensive.

To accomplish his assault, Admiral Spruance created Task Force 50 which consisted of no fewer than six fleet carriers, five light carriers, six battleships and six cruisers, along with 21 destroyers. These were divided into four balanced groups which could provide protection for the amphibious force and support all operations in the Gilbert Islands. The amphibious fleet was divided into two attack forces. Rear-Admiral Turner commanded the naval force carrying 7000 troops of the 27th Infantry Division (Major General RC Smith) which would assault the Makin Atoll supported by three escort carriers. Rear-Admiral Hill was to strike with his force and the 2nd Marine Division (Major General JC Smith) against Tarawa. The special service fleet was to assume a position near the Ellice Islands which was considered the safest point for these essential vessels.

The assault on Makin began on 20 November 1943 against the primary island of Butaritari. The garrison of 800 Japanese troops and 500 laborers gave unexpectedly stiff opposition to the 27th Division. Although the 27th had only 64 killed and 152 wounded, their inexperience prolonged the battle for five full days. Worse still, the battleship *Missouri* suffered a non-combat internal explosion which killed 43 crew-

men and on 24 November the escort carrier *Liscombe Bay* was torpedoed by a Japanese submarine. The carrier sank with 644 of its crew.

The Tarawa Atoll would prove far more difficult to overcome. Its primary island, Betio, possessed the only airfield and was defended by a large garrison of Japanese troops. Betio was fortified with machine-gun positions, pill boxes, barricades, mines and landing obstacles, all supported by the formidable fire power of 8-inch coastal defense guns which had been brought to the island from Singapore. The battle for Tarawa which lasted for approximately 76 hours, would give the Americans their first true glimpse of what lay ahead in the invasions of heavily fortified Japanese-held islands.

The two and one half hour preparatory naval bombardment of Betio on 20 November did little to weaken the island defenses. Naval aircraft failed to arrive on time and the aerial support proved as ineffective as the shelling. It was planned that the Marines should land on three beaches, known as Red 1, 2, and 3, but the coral reef which lay offshore proved an obstacle to the landing craft. The Marines were forced to abandon their craft and wade some 400 yards through chest-deep water under withering fire. Most of the tanks which were to support the invasion were also forced to disembark at the reef where they were easy prey for the Japanese gunners or merely flooded and had to be abandoned. Of the 5000 Marines in the first wave, more than one third never reached the shore. Once on the beaches, progress inland could only be made as Japanese defensive positions were eliminated one by one. As the Marines moved onto the island, they were better able to locate the individual fortifications and naval and air strikes were called against those positions. Even then there were many enemy defenses which had to be cleared with flame throwers and explosives.

By the night of 22 November the Japanese had been pushed to the western edge of the island. From there they attempted a suicidal counterattack which was crushed by the Marines. On 23 November only scattered pockets of resistance remained. The island was secure enough for American aircraft to land on the airstrip. Betio, which was only two miles long and 900 yards wide at its widest point, had cost the lives of more than 1000 Marines with almost three times that number wounded. The Japanese garrison of 4800 troops and laborers had been eliminated but the cost shocked the American people and raised the question of the validity of the island invasions. In fact, though Tarawa had been expensive, the experience gained would stand American forces in good stead.

Nimitz wasted no time. The Gilberts 'rehearsal' was over and plans had been drawn for the invasion of the Marshall Islands. Once the Marshalls fell, the Japanese base at Truk in the Caroline Islands would

be placed in the front line. It had operated in this area as a counterpart to Rabaul and once neutralized the central Pacific would be open to the Allied advance. In February 1944, as MacArthur and Halsey were reaching their objectives in New Guinea and the Solomons, Nimitz ordered the assault of Kwajalein, the Japanese headquarters in the Marshall Islands. With the support of the Fifth Fleet and aircraft from Tarawa, Operation Flintlock began on 31 January. Some 54,000 troops of the 7th Infantry Division and the 4th Marine Division took part in the invasion against a Marshall Islands force of 31,000 Japanese. As at Tarawa, the defenders fought desperately but had no viable air or naval support to lend weight to their efforts. By 22 February the Americans had taken not only Kwajalein but three other islands in the Marshall chain, thus destroying the Japanese hold on the area. Total US casualties were high, but many were wounded and only 372 died at Kwajalein, as opposed to the elimination of the entire Japanese garrison of some 8000 men. As a result of the relatively low fatal casualty figures, 10,000 troops who had been held in reserve were released to reinforce other invasion areas.

The next objective to be gained was the Marianas Islands. The elimination of the Japanese naval base at Truk was the first stage in this advance. On 17 and 18 February, the United States accomplished at Truk what the Japanese had failed to do at Pearl Harbor. Vice-Admiral Marc A Mitscher led a task force which struck at the Japanese base, destroying all vessels caught in the port. Admiral Spruance commanded yet another fleet which intercepted and destroyed Japanese ships attempting to escape to the open sea. When the battle ended, the Japanese had lost 17 combat vessels, including two cruisers and four destroyers plus seven tankers and 19 cargo ships,

desperately needed to maintain the island's defensive strength. The minimal aircover launched in defense of the base was promptly destroyed and by 19 February the base at Truk had been rendered completely useless. In that destruction the United States dropped 30 times the quantity of high explosive that the Japanese used at Pearl Harbor. Thus both Rabaul and Truk had been incapacitated by 1 March 1944. MacArthur could move on to the Dutch East Indies and Nimitz could focus his attention on the Marianas.

After careful preparation the first wave of US Marines hit the beaches of Saipan in the Marianas Islands on the morning of 15 June 1944. As expected the fighting was brutally fierce. The following night a strong Japanese counterattack was repulsed and the 20,000 men of the 2nd and 4th Marine Divisions continued to move inland. The Marianas were the key to Japan's inner defensive perimeter and the Imperial Command ordered the islands held at all cost. Not only would American presence on the Marianas put Allied bombers within range of the Japanese Home Islands, but the loss of the Marianas would open a clear route for MacArthur to swing north to the Philippines. To stop this the Japanese command assembled a formidable fleet. Nine aircraft carriers, five of which were fleet carriers, were distributed between three Japanese task forces with full complements of support vessels. The fleet was commanded by Vice-Admiral Ozawa, a confident and aggressive leader. As they had done so often before, the Japanese command set bait of a small carrier force to draw off the American aircraft while the remainder of the fleet attacked the American vessels. However, American submarines had seen the Japanese fleet and passed full information on to Admiral Spruance. Although he received the information by 18 June, it was out of date and of little use beyond confirming

Left: Admiral Ozawa who
commanded the Japanese
carrier forces during the Battle
of the Philippine Sea.
Center left: Admirals Nimitz
(left) and Spruance at Kwajalein
in February 1944. Spruance was
Ozawa's opponent at the
Philippine Sea.
Far left: Rear-Admiral Kelly
Turner commanded the
amphibious assault units at
Kwajalein and Saipan.
Right: Plans of the Battle of the
Philippine Sea showing the
Japanese attacks (above) and the
American reply.
Below: Marines under heavy
fire during the first assault on
Saipan.

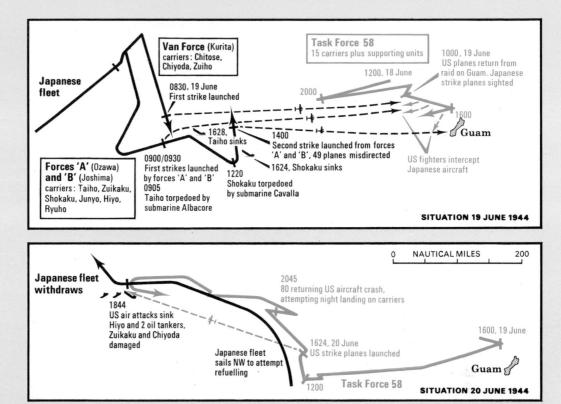

**Japanese
fleet**

Van Force (Kurita)
carriers: Chitose,
Chiyoda, Zuiho

Task Force 58
15 carriers plus supporting units

0830, 19 June
First strike launched

1200, 18 June

2000

1000, 19 June
US planes return from
raid on Guam. Japanese
strike planes sighted

1628,
Taiho sinks

1400

1600

Second strike launched from forces
'A' and 'B', 49 planes misdirected

Guam

Forces 'A' (Ozawa)
and 'B' (Joshima)
carriers: Taiho, Zuikaku,
Shokaku, Junyo, Hiyo,
Ryuho

0900/0930
First strikes launched
by forces 'A' and 'B'
0905
Taiho torpedoed by
submarine Albacore

1220
Shokaku torpedoed
by submarine Cavalla

1624, Shokaku sinks

US fighters intercept
Japanese aircraft

SITUATION 19 JUNE 1944

0   NAUTICAL MILES   200

**Japanese fleet
withdraws**

2045
80 returning US aircraft crash,
attempting night landing on carriers

1844
US air attacks sink
Hiyo and 2 oil tankers,
Zuikaku and Chiyoda
damaged

1600, 19 June

Japanese fleet
sails NW to attempt
refuelling

1624, 20 June
US strike planes launched

Guam

1200

Task Force 58

SITUATION 20 JUNE 1944

that Japanese naval forces were approaching. All available land and carrier reconnaissance aircraft were launched but were unable to locate the Japanese fleet. Ozawa's long range reconnaissance aircraft were more fortunate and by early afternoon on the 18th had located the American carriers.

The distance between the opposing fleets was approximately 400 miles, which placed the Japanese beyond the range of American aircraft. However, the reverse was not true and Ozawa recognized his advantage. He ordered his fleet to maintain its distance intending to begin his attacks at first light on 19 June. Admiral Spruance moved blindly on the evening of 18 June. He had no clear evidence of the location of Ozawa's fleet beyond information supplied by direction-finding stations that the Japanese fleet was approximately 350 miles west-southwest of the carriers of Mitscher's Task Force 58. During that night Spruance and Mitscher argued over the action to be taken. Mitscher favored a dawn attack against the enemy while Spruance remained adamant on protecting the Marianas invasion fleet. The defensive stance was chosen. Spruance ordered his vessels to maneuver to protect the carriers from a possible surface assault and to form an antiaircraft perimeter around them. Any Japanese aircraft which might penetrate that cover would be handled by American aircraft hovering over the vessels and the assault force. Spruance's idea of defense rather than immediate offense brought him much criticism, particularly from Mitscher, but his tactics were employed.

On the morning of 19 June, Japanese reconnaissance planes searched for the exact location of the American fleet. They discovered it and although they were intercepted and eliminated by waiting American fighter patrols the Japanese fleet received their messages and launched their attack. Almost simultaneously an American submarine which had been trailing the Japanese fleet torpedoed and damaged the flagship, the carrier *Taiho*. The sudden submarine attack agitated Japanese gunners who mistook their own aircraft rendezvousing overhead for an American attack. Before they could be stopped they had shot down two of their own aircraft and forced eight others to land with damage. The American fleet was attending to 'business as usual' and after clearing the skies of Japanese land-based planes, American fighters and bombers continued their support against Saipan and the airfield at Guam. While the American aircraft were refueling after these operations, news arrived that a Japanese strike force was closing rapidly. Mitscher knew that he was about to get the fight he had argued for, but instead of it being enacted above the Japanese fleet, it would be fought over his own vessels.

The American carriers launched their aircraft and prepared to defend. Mitscher sent his dive and torpedo bombers to orbit east of the fleet so that the decks might be kept clear for his fighters. The American fighters were sent to intercept the Japanese strike force some 40–60 miles from the fleet. Of the first Japanese wave of 69 aircraft the American pilots shot down 42. The remainder were destroyed by the antiaircraft batteries of Spruance's defensive line. The second Japanese wave of more than 128 aircraft lost at least 100 in the air battle. Twenty broke through to inflict minor damage on the carriers *Wasp* and *Bunker Hill*. The battle ended quickly and of the Japanese force, only 30 aircraft returned to Ozawa's fleet. Although the damage done to the American fleet was minimal, the inexperienced Japanese pilots claimed total victory, exaggerating their successes and causing Admiral Ozawa to make grave errors in his tactical planning. American pilots, however, were justifiably ecstatic. Few American aircraft had been lost and the pilots landed to refuel and rearm to continue the fray. The ease with which they had eliminated the Japanese air attack force caused them to dub the battle 'The Great Marianas Turkey Shoot.' However, the battle was not yet over.

The situation at the Japanese fleet had become grim. On that same afternoon another American submarine torpedoed the carrier *Shokaku*, participant in every major Japanese engagement but Midway. After fighting internal fires for more than three hours, the

remaining crew of the *Shokaku* abandoned the sinking vessel. The flagship *Taiho* suddenly exploded as its crew attempted to vent fumes from the ship. Admiral Ozawa had transferred his staff to another vessel but when the *Taiho* sank only 500 of its more than 2000 crewmen were saved. With two of his front-line carriers out of action the situation might have been considered lost but Ozawa ordered one more air assault against the American fleet. The reports of his pilots indicated that the American fleet was in chaos and he believed that a final attack would bring victory to the Japanese. Ozawa was also laboring under the misconception that the airfield on Guam was operational. He ordered his aircraft to rendezvous with land-based aircraft, strike the American fleet, refuel and rearm at Guam, then strike the Americans once again on their return flight to Ozawa's fleet. Had the Japanese commander known the actual state of affairs, he would undoubtedly have withdrawn. He was an aggressive, not a foolish, commander.

At 1400 hours Japanese aircraft were launched from their fleet. Only half of them would ever find their target, the others becoming disoriented. Of that number, most were destroyed on contact with the American fleet. Worse yet, most of the Japanese pilots who reached Guam found the airfield under attack and were destroyed as they attempted to land on the cratered runways. By nightfall on 19 June the Japanese had lost more than 450 aircraft to American losses of 29, six of which had landed but were declared unserviceable. The Fifth Fleet had achieved a notable victory but Spruance was still criticized for failing to destroy the Japanese carriers. (It was not yet realized that two had already been sunk.) In fact Spruance had judged the Japanese intent and had acted in the best interest of the carrier and invasion fleets. There were admittedly still seven enemy carriers in the area but Spruance's critics failed to appreciate that the 'Turkey Shoot' had nullified the potential of those vessels. Ozawa, now in possession of most of the facts, turned his fleet away to disengage.

It was a victory but Mitscher still desperately wanted to destroy the Japanese carriers. By 1600 hours on 20 June the Japanese fleet had been located and after much debate Spruance gave Mitscher permission to begin an attack. The American aircraft reached their targets and in 20 minutes the carrier *Hiyo* was sinking, the carriers *Zuikaku* and *Chiyoda* were ablaze, and the battleship *Haruna* and cruiser *Maya* were seriously damaged. The 100 aircraft which had been kept operational attempted to defend

Below left: A Hellcat fighter catapulted from the *Monterey*.
Below: Crewmen aboard the *Monterey* relax during a lull.

45

Above: Admiral Marc Mitscher commanded TF.58 during the Battle of the Philippine Sea.

the fleet but when the American pilots withdrew there were only 35 Japanese planes remaining. The Americans lost 17 aircraft in the engagement. The running battle which Ozawa had initiated several days earlier would be one from which the Japanese Navy would never recover and which would seriously hamper their war effort in the months ahead.

Unfortunately for the American aircrew the Battle of the Philippine Sea was not yet ended. Their minimal aircraft losses would be magnified as another enemy, darkness, took its toll. Few of the pilots were trained for night-time operations and they were now faced with the task of landing on their carrier decks in the dark – a situation which produced more anxiety than any number of enemy aircraft. To strike at the Japanese fleet, the American pilots had flown to the limits of their fuel capacity. They had a 300 mile return flight in increasingly poor visibility before reaching their carriers. With the fleet, Mitscher and his staff listened as one pilot after another ran out of fuel and gave his approximate location before setting his aircraft down into the ocean. Many of the pilots exhausted their fuel attempting to locate the fleet until finally orders were given for the carriers and support vessels to turn on all their lights. The commander would risk exposure to Japanese submarines in an effort to save his aircrews. Some 80 of the 200 aircraft were lost in the sea or crashed into the carrier decks. Miraculously in the rescue operations mounted on that night and the following day, all but 49 of the crewmen were rescued. Most of these were lost in the carrier crashes.

The Fifth Fleet was triumphant. Debate on the stance taken by Admiral Spruance would continue, but the fact remained that the Japanese losses would force the Imperial Command to devise new strategies and tactics to counter the offensive power that the United States was bringing to bear. That power was being applied at Saipan even as the naval engagement continued. From 16 June, when the Japanese garrison counterattacked, until 6 July American troops on Saipan fought an arduous battle to eliminate systematically the Japanese defensive positions. The 27th Infantry Division in reserve had to be committed to offset the determined resistance. On 7 July, after their commanders had committed suicide, the defenders again attempted a counterattack that was so intense that even support troops such as cooks and clerks were drawn into the American defense. The attack broken, the 4th Marine Division advanced to Marpi Point at the far end of the island. There American soldiers were horrified by the mass hysteria which had been generated in the civilian population who had taken refuge at Marpi. The Americans could do nothing to prevent many of the civilians leaping to their deaths from the point. By 9 July the island was considered secure. Saipan had cost 3500 American lives with 9000 wounded and more than 700 missing. Japanese losses were estimated at 24–26,000.

On 19 July the American battleships began the bombardment of Guam that would destroy the airfield to which Admiral Ozawa was sending his aircraft. Two days later the invasion began as the 3rd Marine Division, the 1st Marine Brigade and finally the 77th Infantry Division moved to the two designated beaches. For four days the beachhead struggle continued, until on 25 July the Japanese launched what was becoming the all too familiar *Banzai* suicidal charge. Although several American positions fell, the 3rd Marine Division was able to break the attack killing 3500 Japanese troops, 95 percent of the attacking force. The charge cost the Marines 166 dead, 645 wounded and 34 missing, which would constitute most of the losses for the entire Guam invasion. From that point on, the Japanese would be unable to withstand the steady American advance. By 10 August all organized resistance on the island was eliminated. The most peculiar aspect of the battle for Guam would be seen 16 years later when a Japanese soldier was discovered living in the jungle. Convinced that the war was still going on, it took a great deal of persuasion before he surrendered.

The final phase of the battle for the Marianas was the capture of Tinian. That effort lasted from 24 July until 1 August, though the heaviest fighting occurred during the first 24 hours of the invasion. It was a more rapid but by no means less costly victory for the 2nd and 4th Marine Divisions, with 400 killed and 2000 wounded. Japanese losses numbered at least 10,000. By mid August the Marianas were secured. The combined land and naval battles had devastated the Japanese strength and had cost them a crucial strategic perimeter defense. Once repaired, the islands' five airfields would be the base for the B-29 Superfortress bombers which would strike at the cities of Japan. Tinian was destined to be remembered as the base from which the *Enola Gay* began its flight to Hiroshima.

7 RETURN TO THE PHILIPPINES

With the Marianas in American hands and the Caroline Islands virtually secured, the way was clear for MacArthur's Southwest Pacific Command and Halsey's South Pacific Command to unite for the drive to the Philippines. Together they decided to begin by capturing Leyte. In adopting this plan, the Japanese defenses in the Dutch East Indies, Borneo and the Celebes would be ignored. It was a bold scheme but MacArthur and Halsey were convinced that those bases posed no potential threat. Recent air and naval engagements had illustrated the weaknesses of the Japanese. Without means to maneuver or transport their troops from the East Indies, the Japanese forces there were useless. Once Leyte and then, in December 1944 Mindoro, were taken they were to become bases for the American heavy bombers which would support MacArthur's invasion of the primary island, Luzon, which held the capital Manila.

However, three more support bases had to be established before MacArthur's return to the Philippines could be accomplished. The islands of Peleliu in the Palau Atoll and Morotai in the Caroline Islands were essential for their airbases. Although Japanese resistance was fierce, particularly at Peleliu, the islands were taken with relatively little difficulty. The island of Ulithi in the Carolines was also taken and would serve as a fleet anchorage and base for the Philippine invasion forces.

American troops landed on Leyte on 20 October 1944 and in response the Japanese began preparations for a naval battle which would have a major effect on the outcome of the Philippine campaign. The Japanese divided their naval forces into three primary groups for their effort to repulse the invasion. Once again a carrier task force was used to lure the American fleet carriers away so that the Japanese surface fleet, in two main groups, could direct its full weight against MacArthur's invasion fleet at Leyte.

One of the battle fleets approached Leyte Gulf via the Surigao Straits. Rear-Admiral Jesse B Oldendorf who had been present at the first major surface battle in the Pacific, as fate would have it, would also be present at the last. His naval squadron was patrolling the area through which the Japanese fleet advanced. As the Japanese vessels moved through the strait in single file, Oldendorf struck with six battleships, three heavy cruisers and two sections of light cruisers. He had positioned several groups of torpedo boats on either side of the strait with orders to harass the approaching enemy fleet so that he could engage it on his own terms. The torpedo boats would also be responsible for dealing with damaged Japanese vessels or those attempting to break off from the battle. The Japanese, travelling at night, were unaware of the American presence. Oldendorf, in traditional naval style, 'crossed the T' of Vice-Admiral Nishimura's fleet. From a distance of approximately eight miles he delivered the full broadside capability of his battle fleet into the Japanese line. In that crossed T formation he was able to bring his maximum firepower to bear while the Japanese found it impossible to respond. It was a swift and easy victory in which Oldendorf's

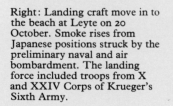

Right: Landing craft move in to the beach at Leyte on 20 October. Smoke rises from Japanese positions struck by the preliminary naval and air bombardment. The landing force included troops from X and XXIV Corps of Krueger's Sixth Army.

vessels suffered only minor damage. The Japanese fleet retreated having been reduced to one cruiser and one destroyer.

The second Japanese task force, led by Admiral Kurita, was also on a course for Leyte Gulf to attack MacArthur's invasion fleet. American submarines sank three heavy cruisers while the pilots from Mitscher's Task Force 38 sank a battleship of this fleet while it was still in the Sibuyan Sea. By the time Halsey received information on the engagement he believed that the aircraft and submarines had caused such damage that the Japanese task force would certainly be withdrawing. In any event the lure of the Japanese carriers, which had been sent to bait him, proved too great a challenge to ignore. The error would prove costly. Admiral Kurita had a force of no less than four battleships, six heavy cruisers and some dozen destroyers remaining and although he had suffered high casualties, he was not yet beaten. His force passed through the San Bernardino Straits at 2400 hours on 24 October. From there he proceeded toward Leyte Gulf. The American command was thrown into confusion. Kurita continued to advance and found an escort carrier group led by Admiral CF Sprague and made up of six escort carriers and seven small destroyers. These escort carriers carried only 30 aircraft each and were slow and lightly armed. Their function had been to give close air support to the invasion, not to engage in combat with an enemy

Above: An American destroyer lays a smokescreen off Leyte.
Above right: A Japanese survivor of the Surigao Strait battle.
Below: The destroyer *Downes* during a bombardment operation.

surface fleet. The only other vessels with which Sprague could defend the invasion force were three destroyers and four destroyer escorts which did not carry torpedoes. The odds were clearly against him.

On the morning of 25 October Sprague's vessels engaged the Japanese task force near Samar Island, for which the battle would be named. Rain and a smoke screen laid by the destroyers gave some aid to the American vessels. What few aircraft Sprague possessed tried desperately to inflict damage on the Japanese ships but they were unequal to the task. He was forced to order them to refuel on Leyte, the only serviceable airfield, so that he would not have to expose his carriers by maneuvering into the wind to receive the aircraft. Thirty minutes after the enemy was sighted, Sprague sent a desperate message reporting that the enemy was closing fast and that the volume of fire was devastating. He also stated regretfully that he did not think he could slow the Japanese fleet let alone stop its advance. At that point three American destroyers, the *Johnston, Hoel,* and the *Samuel B. Roberts* executed some of the most heroic naval actions seen in the Pacific.

The USS *Johnston* had been in commission for less than one year. Its captain, Commander Ernest E Evans, a full-blooded Cherokee Indian, had informed his crew at the outset that theirs was a fighting vessel and fight it would. As the Japanese fleet closed on the carriers, Evans maneuvered his ship directly in their path. For more than 20 minutes he screened the American carriers, taking the full fire of the Japanese vessels. His own 5-inch guns were unable to bridge the distance to the Japanese ships. When the enemy fleet entered his range Evans' crew sent off 200 rounds and 10 torpedoes, primarily at the cruiser *Kumano,* which would later sink.

However the *Johnston* had taken three critical hits which eliminated one of its two main engines and cut the power for steering the vessel and aiming the 5-inch guns. Both ship and guns had to be controlled manually, a by no means simple task, but the USS *Johnston* was not defeated. The escort carrier *Gambier Bay* was being engaged by a Japanese cruiser and battleship. Evans maneuvered his vessel between them in an effort to draw fire away from the carrier. From there he proceeded to engage a full Japanese destroyer flotilla of at least six vessels which were closing on the *Gambier Bay* from another direction. Finally by 1015 hours 25 October the *Johnston* was sunk, its power and ammunition gone. Of its 327-man crew only one third survived. Evans himself was among those killed. Although the *Johnston* has been singled out here the *Hoel* and *Samuel B. Roberts* fought with similar bravery and were also lost.

Admiral Kurita had the upper hand but his losses against so small an American naval and air force made him consider the battle lost. He withdrew toward the San Bernardino Straits. Admiral Sprague had

miraculously won the engagement by default. He lost five vessels, two of them escort carriers, one of which was sunk when a Japanese aircraft dived directly into it. The battle had done much to add to the disintegrating morale and capability of the Japanese Navy. Though destroyers and barges would continue to bring reinforcements for the Japanese armies, Japanese naval power was no longer an effective threat.

The Battle of Samar Island and the sinking of one of the American carriers introduced the latest, most desperate of Japanese tactics, the Kamikaze. After the Marianas engagement, most of the remaining experienced Japanese pilots were withdrawn to Japan to protect the Home Islands. Although their numbers were few, it was believed that they could serve as the nucleus of the air defense of Japan. Most other pilots were mere novices. It would take precious time to train them properly in the methods of air tactics; time which the Japanese did not have. Desperate measures were called for and the Kamikaze, was born. Kamikaze means Divine Wind and recalls a famous historical Japanese victory. The young men who joined its ranks were taught only two basic flight techniques: how to take off and how to crash into a naval vessel to do the most damage. The Kamikaze would become the nightmare of the American naval personnel. Their fanatical determination made it virtually impossible to stop them with conventional air and naval defense tactics. Kamikaze attacks would wreak more damage on American task forces than any of the previous surface engagements. Perhaps most important, when combined with the Banzai land attack psychology, the Kamikaze indicated the lengths to which the Japanese intended to go to stop the American advance

Above: General Walter Krueger (left) and Admiral Kinkaid aboard a headquarters ship.
Right: A Japanese suicide plane crashes after being hit by AA fire during the Leyte Gulf operation.
Below: Three GIs move cautiously through a Luzon village on the look out for snipers.

toward the Japanese Home Islands.

Once Leyte was considered relatively secure, MacArthur turned his attention toward Luzon, the main objective. It was a controversial issue. The Japanese defenses on Luzon were believed to be well organized and it was estimated that the garrison was 250,000 strong. There were many who argued that if the United States was prepared to expend so many lives and so much effort, it should be directed against a more important strategic objective such as Formosa. From Formosa the United States could have land-based aircraft operating even closer to the Japanese Home Islands. But the recapture of Luzon obsessed MacArthur. He had been forced to abandon the Philippines in the opening months of the war but he had sworn to return and he would not go back on his word. Added to that was the fact that the men of his original Philippine command, as well as many Philippine citizens, were prisoners of war on Luzon. MacArthur wanted to liberate 'his army and his people.' It was a volatile situation. Although Formosa was indeed a most important objective, there were those on the American Joint Chiefs of Staff who felt that it was not outside the realm of possibility for MacArthur flagrantly to disregard instructions to bypass Luzon. MacArthur not only knew how to win battles; he was also an expert at manipulating the news media. He would certainly have made the prisoners of war an issue if ordered to advance to Formosa. Such a controversy would have an unpleasant effect on the Roosevelt administration's image of strength, and possibly a detrimental effect on the war effort. The fact that the Luzon-Formosa issue was being considered in October 1944, just prior to the Presidential elections, gave added incentive for avoiding a confrontation which might cause Roosevelt's credibility to suffer.

Finally at the end of November the plans to invade Luzon were officially approved and MacArthur was able to set an invasion date of 9 January 1945. To accomplish the invasion he had General Walter Krueger's Sixth Army of more than 200,000 men. This army had an enormous reserve which could reach the island in a matter of days if needed. Admiral Halsey's Third Fleet, with its powerful carrier task force was ready to give air and naval support to the invasion and neutralize any support the Japanese might attempt to send from Formosa. Vice-Admiral Thomas C Kinkaid's Seventh Fleet, with its 850 combat, transport, and support vessels, would also be called upon to support the operations. As if this were not enough General George Kenney's Fifth Air Force with bases on Mindoro and Leyte could maintain bomber pressure on Luzon and could strike at designated strategic targets in the area.

Against all of this the Japanese had more than 250,000 troops but they were in fact poorly organized, deployed and led. There were very few Japanese naval

vessels protecting the waters around Luzon and fewer than 150 combat aircraft were on the island. The American fear of meeting veteran Japanese troops was unfounded as most of them had been drawn off to reinforce the preceding island engagements. Those remaining were second-line troops with little if any combat experience. Only a few elite Japanese naval landing troops, the equivalent of Marine shock troops, were present to give backbone to the Japanese garrison.

From the time the American invasion force left Leyte on 2 January until the invasion of Luzon, Kamikaze aircraft succeeded in damaging or destroying at least a dozen Allied vessels and caused more than 1000 casualties. Two days prior to the invasion aircraft from Halsey's fleet destroyed what remained of the Japanese airpower in the Philippines, but long range Kamikaze attacks continued. Finally at 0930 hours on 9 January the Sixth Army landed on the southern beaches at Lingayen Gulf, the site used by the Japanese when they invaded the island more than four years earlier. The landing was accomplished without opposition and by the end of that day more than 68,000 American troops had established a beachhead 17 miles wide and four miles deep. General MacArthur joined his men on the beach as he had done at Leyte. The lack of opposition puzzled but gratified the

American command. MacArthur immediately swung out in two directions. General Oscar Griswold's XIV Corps proceeded south toward Manila while General Innis P Swift's I Corps moved north toward what was believed to be the main concentration of the Japanese Fourteenth Area Army. Swift's corps met heavy resistance but by 28 January had successfully captured the key road junction in the Cabaruan Hills. At the same time, Griswold's Corps was being held up not by enemy resistance but by the joyous Philippine civilians whose enthusiasm impeded the corps' progress across the island. Griswold continued to advance cautiously, encountering no enemy resistance and fearing that he was being drawn into a trap. On 17 January MacArthur was forced to order Griswold to increase his pace. He was impatient for the capture of Manila and Clark Field, a coup which would help provide air support for operations throughout the island. He was equally anxious that the prisoners of war in that area be released as quickly as possible.

On 23 January Griswold's XIV Corps finally encountered the enemy. A 30,000-man Japanese defense had been established to hold Clark Field. For more than 72 hours the Americans probed the defenses. Victory was won on 27 January only after the slow, arduous task of eliminating the Japanese positions with demolitions and flame throwers was completed.

With Clark Field securely in American hands, Griswold's forces moved on toward Manila by 31 January. During this time American Rangers and Philippine guerrillas made their first rescue of 500 Allied prisoners at Cabanatuan. They executed their raid at night and though constantly pursued, successfully reached the American lines with their grateful charges. At the same time, the United States XI Corps commanded by General Charles P Hall landed unopposed on the west coast of Luzon just north of the Bataan Peninsula, capturing the nearby airfield and naval installation. On 31 January also, units of the 11th Airborne Division made an assault landing at Nasugbu, south of Manila but met heavy resistance when they tried to advance inland to the capital. They were, however, reinforced by a parachute drop.

Manila could now be assaulted from all sides. One of MacArthur's primary targets within the capital was Santo Tomas University in the northern sector of the city. The university had served as the prison for more than 35,000 Allied civilians captured when the Philippines were first invaded. Defending Manila were some 17,000 troops of the elite naval forces. Their staunch resistance turned the battle for the capital into a vicious street war. It was not until 3 March that the city was actually taken, at a cost of more than 1000

American troops killed and 6000 wounded. Worse still, some 100,000 Philippine civilians caught in the bitter struggle lost their lives, many of whom were said to have been slain by the Japanese in the last desperate hours of the battle. With Manila recaptured, MacArthur established a new government and set about eliminating all pockets of Japanese resistance on Manila Bay and Corregidor. That tiny island, which had once been MacArthur's headquarters, was the last bastion of Japanese resistance in the area and MacArthur was determined to crush it. Corregidor fell at a cost of another 1000 American lives. Of the 5000 Japanese defenders only 19 survived. MacArthur had truly returned. Curiously, although much of Manila was destroyed by bombing raids and the ground battles, the local brewery owned by General MacArthur was never once struck or damaged.

By the end of March the fighting on Luzon was virtually confined to the northern end of the island. Around 170,000 Japanese troops would continue to hold out there until the end of the war. Many died of malnutrition and disease but they refused to surrender, determined to keep large numbers of American troops immobilized to counter their potential threat. Sporadic fighting on the other Philippine Islands continued until the end of the war. Fewer than 25 percent of the total Japanese Luzon force of 250,000 would survive, while American casualties totalled 8000 killed and over 30,000 wounded – with another 2000 lost in Kamikaze attacks.

Left: Admiral Kinkaid looks out over the Luzon invasion fleet.
Below: A view of bomb damage in Baguio taken in April 1945. The US forces had overwhelming air support in the Philippines.

8 IWO JIMA AND OKINAWA

Before the Philippines had been taken the American command looked forward to an objective which Nimitz felt was critical for the United States. Since 1943 he had been planning the means by which the United States could take the island of Iwo Jima. This was one island which could not be bypassed.

Since the Americans had taken Saipan, Guam and Tinian the B-29 bombers had begun flying missions over Japan. They faced a major problem, however. Their flights from those islands meant a round trip of some 3000 miles. It was obvious that a midway staging site would be useful. On the one hand the B-29s needed fighter protection to escort them over Japan. Although defensive Japanese air crews were not of the highest caliber, their aircraft had been modified for increased firepower and defensive strength. They could absorb much more punishment than the B-29 gunners could usually deliver and consequently the bombers were taking more losses than were acceptable. The Japanese air force had also introduced a new tactic by late 1944. Kamikaze pilots were not only attacking American vessels but had begun to use their suicide tactics in the air. Japanese pilots, lacking the experience and skill to shoot American aircraft from the skies, began crashing their fighters into American bombers. One fighter for one bomber was considered an advantageous trade.

Iwo Jima represented the best possible site for American fighter bases. It was well positioned only 660 miles from the Japanese main islands. A base at Iwo Jima would also provide the American bombers with an emergency airfield. Disabled bombers which were unable to make the long flight back to the Marianas could land there. The other important factor was that Iwo Jima had long been a vital link in Japan's air defense. There were two airfields on the island, with a third under construction, from which Japanese air assaults were launched or aircraft made ready for flights to more distant perimeter islands.

Finally, and not of least importance, Iwo Jima was the first island in the chain of Japanese Home Islands. It was a part of the Empire and had always been under Japan's governmental control. It was believed that the capture of the island would be a serious psychological blow to the Japanese people. As a part of Japan, Nimitz and Marine Corps General Smith viewed Iwo Jima as a testing ground to measure the degree of opposition the Americans could expect when the actual invasion of the primary islands of Japan began. The Japanese resistance throughout the Pacific islands had become legendary. Their willingness to die to a man in defense of the perimeter bases made them the most formidable of foes. This factor filled American strategists with dread. If the Japanese were willing to fight so fanatically on the perimeter, how much more determined would they be when Japan itself was threatened? The invasion of Iwo Jima would be the meter for gauging the casualties to be anticipated in a future invasion of Japan.

The task of invading Iwo Jima was given to the veteran V Amphibious Corps of Nimitz's Fifth Fleet. Three divisions were chosen. The 4th Marine Division, under Major General Clifton B Cates was perhaps the most experienced in all the Pacific, having made its reputation at Saipan and Tinian. The 5th Marine Division, commanded by Major General Keller E Rockey, which shared many honors with the 4th Division, was also selected. However this division had suffered enormous casualties with only 40 percent of the men being actual combat veterans. The remaining 60 percent were replacements, many of whom would see their first action at Iwo Jima. The final assault force was the 3rd Marine Division, Major General Graves B Erskine commanding, which would be held offshore as an initial reserve. This order was not well received by the division. The Marines well knew that troop transports were among the favored targets for Kamikazes. They considered themselves helpless against that enemy and would have preferred to take their chances on the beaches.

At the beginning of November 1944 American combat vessels and aircraft began bombarding Iwo Jima in an effort to neutralize the Japanese heavy artillery and disorganize the defenses of the island. By February 1945 the Navy and Air Corps assured the invasion commanders that at least 80 percent of the island's defenses were destroyed and except for the garrison troops, the Marines should have little difficulty with the invasion. This intelligence was based mostly on the opinion of the Air Corps and Navy command, which did not believe that any defensive structures could withstand the bombardment which had been

Above: Casualties and debris on the beach at Iwo Jima.
Top left: Marines being briefed before the Iwo Jima landing.
Top right: Japanese Kamikaze pilots preparing for an attack.

directed at Iwo Jima. On 17 February 1945, during the continued bombardment, American frogmen made their way to the island to set demolition charges on obstructions to the Marines' avenues of approach. They were also to conduct a reconnaissance of the area to determine the exact nature of the defenses which the Marines would encounter. The Japanese spotted the frogmen and, believing that the invasion had begun, opened fire with their heavy guns. Naval gunners marked the positions and began to destroy them systematically. Of the more than 200 frogmen who went ashore some 170 were casualties. On their return they told a completely different story to the one intelligence had given earlier. Although the primary beach defenses appeared to be vacant the defensive works and positions they had seen were in excellent condition. The frogmen warned that it was extremely likely that the Japanese had more to offer in defense than had been believed.

In spite of this warning the invasion proceeded as planned. On the morning of 19 February eight Marine battalions made their way ashore. It took them 45 minutes to cross the 4000 yards from their transports to the beaches. During that time they were exposed to

the bunkers and pillboxes which had wreaked havoc on the Marines. By the end of that first day more than 30,000 Marines had landed and although casualties were high, the lower neck of the island and part of an airfield had been secured.

The following day the Marines turned south and gained a foothold on Mount Suribachi. Three days later, after a bitter struggle which employed both men and tanks armed with flame throwers, this highest point on the island was finally taken. A 40-man patrol of Marines reached the summit and raised the American flag. This was by no means an indication that the island was taken, but from their positions the Marines saw the flag and it gave them a much needed morale boost. For the next 48 hours the Marines pushed into the island, making progress only by a few yards at a time. It had become obvious to the invasion commanders that the entire island was nothing more than a honeycombed bunker. Perhaps 1000 positions were linked by underground passages which permitted the enemy to escape as Marines attempted to clear their positions. The passage systems meant that the Marines often found themselves under attack from

Left: Marines on Iwo Jima consult their map in order to signal the position of a Japanese machine-gun emplacement to their supporting artillery. The Japanese positions were generally well concealed and fortified.

Above left: Marine wiremen at work on telephone lines on Iwo Jima. This photograph was taken on 4 March near the end of the battle.

one of the heaviest barrages seen in the Pacific. As they reached the beaches at 0900 hours they met only sporadic resistance. For some 20 minutes the Japanese allowed them to move inland but about 300 yards from the water the Japanese trap was sprung. These were defensive positions which the frogmen had not seen. The Japanese were learning their lessons as the Americans made their island-hopping invasions and had laid their defenses inland where the naval guns could not effectively strike them without also striking the landing forces. Marine descriptions of the situation depicted a 'hell itself.' However, for the next 90 minutes the Marine battalions continued to land. Their heavy support, including tanks and bulldozers, also arrived on the shore. The arrival of the tanks was especially welcomed as they were able to deal with

the front and rear. After passing defenses that they had assumed were cleared of enemy troops the Marines advanced only to find that the Japanese had returned and were now behind them.

It was a desperate situation. The 3rd Division was landed on 25 February by which time American casualties were already very high, perhaps equal to those being suffered by the Japanese. Many units had their combat strength cut well below 50 percent. On 9 March the Marines finally broke through on the northeast shore of Iwo Jima. Withstanding several Banzai attacks, after which more than 700 Japanese dead were counted, the 3rd Division and sections of the 4th Marines held the position. They were heartened by the sight of American bombers and fighters launching from one of the airfields on the island.

For another week the Marines continued to assault Japanese positions. Finally on 26 March the island was considered secured after the last desperate attack of the 300 remaining Japanese troops had been beaten off. The price of securing Iwo Jima had been high. Of the estimated 23,000 Japanese defenders only 1000 were taken prisoner, and most of those only because they were seriously wounded. For the Americans, nearly 7000 were dead. An even more frightening statistic was that of combat fatigue victims. At least 3000 men suffered complete breakdowns under the strain of the combat to which they were exposed. Also in that 36 days of fighting the United States' highest decoration, the Congressional Medal of Honor, was given to 24 men. The American strategist who looked at these statistics had much to consider. On the basis of events on Iwo Jima the cost in men and materiel necessary to invade Japan would be phenomenal. But there was a bright aspect. By 7 April there were more than 100 P-51 long-range fighter aircraft flying from Iwo Jima's three airfields protecting the B-29s over Japan, and over the next three months almost 1000 of the bombers and their crews would be saved because Iwo Jima's airfields were there to accept their disabled planes. The cost was high but Iwo Jima repeatedly proved its value to the United States.

The last major island which the Americans had to conquer in their progress toward Japan was Okinawa. Like Iwo Jima, Okinawa had its own particular worth. Not only did it have excellent airfields, more of which could be built on the available terrain, but Okinawa was only 325 miles from Japan proper. It also had several natural bays and harbors which would make excellent naval bases for the assembly of American forces for the invasion of Japan. Okinawa was large enough to support the several million men that the United States and its allies thought would be needed for that invasion. Those forces would be less vulnerable to Kamikaze attacks on a land base than they would have been had they been forced to wait at sea. Okinawa had to be taken as soon as possible to be prepared for the role which the United States intended it to play. It would not be a pleasant task. The local defense was the Thirty-second Japanese Army with a total force of 80,000 men, supported by some 20,000 loyal Okinawan citizens. Okinawa had also received reinforcements from the elite units which had been fighting in China and Manchuria. As they prepared to defend this last bastion before their homeland was attacked, the Japanese Imperial Command issued a statement which was taken as the battle slogan of the Thirty-second Army: 'One plane for one warship, one boat for one ship, one man for one tank, one man for every 10 of the enemy.' The Kamikaze spirit had spread throughout the Japanese military. Their only hope was to make the war so costly for the Americans that an honorable peace could be made before the homeland was invaded.

Above: Admiral Raymond Spruance pictured in April 1945 during the Okinawa operation. Spruance and Halsey alternated in command of the principal US naval forces in the Pacific, known as Fifth Fleet when Spruance commanded, and as Third Fleet under Halsey.

Above: Vice-Admiral Oldendorf pictured aboard the battleship *Tennessee* in August 1945 off Okinawa. Oldendorf commanded the battleship bombardment force in the Okinawa operation. He also led the US forces in the Surigao Strait battle.

Admiral Nimitz designated Spruance's Fifth Fleet as the primary support and assistance for the invasion of Okinawa. It seemed fitting that the Fifth Fleet, which had fought its way across the Central Pacific, should be given the right to participate in the final battles of the war. The invasion forces were under the command of General Simon B Buckner, a popular hero after his campaign with American forces in the Aleutian Islands. He was considered a man who knew how to get a job done without needlessly sacrificing the lives of his troops. This aspect made Buckner the most logical choice for the command. The invasion planners knew that casualties would be enormous and they wanted a man who would not be blamed for senseless waste of American men. Under Buckner was a force consisting of the XXIV Corps commanded by Major General John R Hodge, an old Army regular, and the II Amphibious Corps under Major General Roy Geiger, USMC. Each of these corps had two divisions in the front line and Buckner held a reserve of three divisions. In total Buckner's Tenth Army had some 180,000 men. Before the battle for Okinawa was over the troops employed would number 500,000.

On 1 April 1945 the invasion began. It was Easter Sunday, but most of the troops recognized it more as April Fools Day, for that was what they thought they must be to assault Okinawa. Buckner expected that the numbers of defenders would mean that the entire island would be fanatically defended, causing 50–75 percent casualties to his forces before they ever reached the beaches. However, as the invasion got under way little opposition was met. The troops expected another trap similar to that found on Iwo

Jima but as they continued to advance, that fear passed. American troops moved from the beaches rapidly, and in the first day more than 50,000 men were landed encountering nothing more than occasional sniper fire. There was so little harassment that engineers and Seabees began immediately to service the two airfields taken so that American aircraft could put them to use.

During those first days the main combat victory was not on land but at sea. On 7 April the Japanese attempted the most desperate suicidal mission to date. The battleship *Yamato*, the pride of the Japanese Navy, was sent with only enough fuel to reach Okinawa on a mission to destroy the American fleet. Instead the giant battleship was caught by aircraft from Mitscher's Task Force 58 and sunk while still more than 270 miles from Okinawa. The largest battleship seen until that time was destroyed without ever actually striking a blow for Japan.

Although he was surprised by the lack of resistance on Okinawa, Buckner decided to grasp as much of the island as he could. He sent the II Amphibious Corps north and by 9 April the 6th Marine Division had captured a 20-mile section of the island. At the same time XXIV Corps began pushing south where they ultimately found the main forces of the Japanese Thirty-second Army. It seemed that the Japanese commander had decided that the cliffs on that sector of the island were his most advantageous point of defense. This region, approximately 10 miles long and five miles wide, would become some of the most costly territory of the war. The Japanese had established a line behind the Shuri Castle and had built a defense that they believed the Americans could never break. As at Iwo Jima, the mountainous region was honeycombed with caves, passages and fortified defensive structures. As the northern section of the island was secured, Buckner sent XXIV Corps reinforced by reserve divisions to lay siege to the Japanese army's defenses. To aid the attack he added the support of 324 artillery pieces, the naval guns from six battleships, six cruisers and six destroyers, and a force of more than 600 Marine and Navy aircraft. On 9 April the assault was opened with a 40-minute barrage which used more than 20,000 rounds of ammunition. When it subsided the XXIV Corps advanced but the Japanese defensive line could not be breached. The 1st Marine Division was added to the assault and several days later the 6th Marine Division moved from the north to add its weight, but to no avail.

Although they had withstood all that the Americans had thrown against them, the Japanese commander finally ordered a counterattack on 2 May. The attack was well planned and even included a small amphibious assault using barges which had been hidden on the southern edge of the island. The Japanese did not have enough extra support to break the American lines and more than 5000 Japanese troops died in the attempt. One phase of the attack did succeed. Small vessels of every type launched a suicidal attack on the American support fleet. This attack was coupled with Kamikaze attacks which flew from grass airfields on the southern tip of the island. All together the suicide raids managed to damage 14 and sink four American vessels.

On 11 May the Americans again assaulted the defensive fortifications. Their effort was futile and their mood was not helped by witnessing more than 150 Kamikaze aircraft striking against the American fleet. The carrier *Bunker Hill* was hit by two Japanese aircraft which forced Admiral Mitscher to transfer his staff to the *Enterprise*. Three days later that vessel was also hit, forcing him to move his command headquarters to yet another ship. By the end of May Buckner had come to the grim realization that after more than six weeks of fighting his troops were covering only an average of 100 yards per day with more than 20,000 casualties. Although on 29 May the 1st Marines captured the Shuri Castle the Japanese showed no signs of weakening. In the first days of June an amphibious assault was made on the small Oruku Peninsula in the hope of flanking a Japanese stronghold, but little was actually accomplished. Two weeks later American troops attacked once again and finally on 17 and 18 June they began to see some progress. On 19 June the first actual display of weakness came when Japanese troops, with their backs to the sea, began to surrender. In other areas the Japanese continued to struggle fiercely, literally dying by the thousands. As fate would have it General Buckner would not live to see the signs that the Japanese would soon be defeated. On 18 June while assessing the situation from a forward observation point he was killed by an artillery round. He was two miles and four days short of his long awaited goal.

On 21 June the Japanese commanders on Okinawa committed suicide rather than surrender. The following morning Japanese resistance ended. Eighty-two days of fighting had cost the Japanese 110,000 men, almost all of the garrison. Of the 1900 suicidal attacks made on the American ships, the casualties caused were 16 Allied or American vessels sunk and 150 damaged. When compared to Iwo Jima, where far fewer Kamikaze attacks were made, the statistics indicated the frightening lengths to which the Japanese would go to destroy the American threat. The American Tenth Army's casualties were more than 8000 killed, 32,000 wounded and another 26,000 dead or injured from non-combat causes. Naval casualties were listed at approximately 10,000, with around half of those being fatalities from the Kamikaze raids. The United States had the naval and air base it needed to launch the invasion of Japan, but the losses which had been sustained in preparation for that invasion made many fervently hope that some other means for the defeat of the Japanese would be found.

Right: A Grumman Avenger moves in to attack Japanese positions on Okinawa. Note underwing rockets and open bomb doors.
Bottom left: Japanese soldiers surrender to a Marine of the 6th Division on Okinawa.
Bottom right: Major General Lemuel C Shepherd plans the next move for his 6th Marine Division during the battle for Okinawa.
Below: Heavily armed Marines advance inland on the first day of the Okinawa battle. The Marine in the center carries a flame thrower.

9 THE ECLIPSE OF THE RISING SUN

While the battle for Okinawa was raging and the war in Europe was in its final days the United States was dealt a bitter blow. On 12 April 1945 after leading the American people through the Great Depression era and through a war the likes of which had never been seen, President Franklin Delano Roosevelt died of a cerebral hemorrhage. His health had never been good. He had been crippled since 1921, able to walk only with artificial support but his strength as a leader had made him one of the most powerful men of his time. The United States mourned his loss as Vice-President Harry S Truman took the reins of government. Truman, like most Vice-Presidents, had been given some duties and projects but was kept in the dark about important matters discussed and agreed upon by Roosevelt in the many negotiations and conferences that had taken place. In fact, throughout the course of the war Roosevelt had briefed Truman only twice on war matters. It was for this reason that Truman, although verbally committed to pursuing Roosevelt's programs, did not feel obliged to maintain the dead President's policies.

When Truman took office he faced several problems. The war in Europe was almost over and he would have to be involved in negotiating a peace. But the war with Japan was still going on and the final direction of that war effort would have to be decided upon. Most importantly, when Truman took office he had never been told of the Manhattan Project – the development of the first atomic weapon. That issue would place one of the gravest decisions of the twentieth century, perhaps in the history of mankind, on Truman's shoulders.

The new President also had problems competing with the shadow of his predecessor. He was treated as though he was an outsider by the men of his own government and as a minor actor in the drama that Churchill and Stalin were directing. Although the initial days did not augur well for him, Truman decided that he was going to set policy in his own particular fashion.

One factor which had to be taken into account was the progress of the strategic bombing campaign being flown by bombers from the Marianas and Iwo Jima. As in Europe, the United States believed that massive bombing could effectively destroy the enemy's will to

fight. Day after day from the beginning of 1945 large flights of American bombers flew missions over Japan. In one raid alone 96 percent of Tokyo was destroyed by incendiary bombs. Major General Curtis LeMay, who commanded the American bombers in the Marianas, believed that civilian areas as well as industrial targets should be destroyed. Only this would convince the Japanese people that resistance would ultimately mean the end of their society. There were many who criticized these tactics as a form of genocidal warfare against the Japanese people, and although rescued prisoners of war explained that their treatment had become more brutal in retaliation for the bombings, the campaign continued.

The B-29 was the most effective weapon in the bombing strategy. One bomber could drop 40 clusters of 38 incendiary bombs which could virtually obliterate everything in an area of 16 acres. On 9 March the devastation of the great Tokyo Raid would prove this and Americans would later learn that this fire raid caused more casualties than either of the atomic bombs. Nine days after the great Tokyo Raid the Japanese cities of Kobe, Nagoya and Osaka were similarly destroyed. The list of target sites continued to grow. It was a total air war against large populated areas as well as the minor airfields, harbors and smaller villages which had previously been considered off-limits to air attacks. In another phase of the air war, mines were laid in the waters off Japan's coastlines. These mines accounted for the loss of more than 1,200,000 tons of Japanese shipping and brought war transport between the islands virtually to a halt. By June 1945 the Japanese air defense had been reduced to such a minimal level that the United States began

announcing its raids in advance to add propaganda to the claims that the Japanese were beaten. In many areas American bombers dropped pamphlets instead of bombs urging the Japanese to give up the senseless struggle.

The devastation had been tremendous and civilian morale was beginning to crack. No longer could the Imperial Command or the government maintain strict order within society. After the great Tokyo Raid some 8,500,000 civilians fled the city to take refuge in the surrounding mountains and countryside. Production ground to a halt, reducing industrial productivity to less than 5 percent of its previous level. Raw materials could only be brought into Japan by submarines and since they carried so little cargo, the effort was not even worth the fuel expended by the submarines. The Imperial Command was forced to begin considering the Allies' surrender demands but they continued to call for the Japanese people to fight to the last man, woman and child in defense of the homeland and the Emperor. Officially, the Japanese leaders refused to consider the American peace offers. The United States had no choice but to continue to apply heavy pressure from the air.

Nimitz was now faced with putting into operation his plans for the invasion of Japan. Since late 1943 he had been working with the Joint Chiefs of Staff on Operation Olympic, the two-phase invasion strategy. The operation called for one American force to strike into China near Ningpo to establish staging facilities there while a more important attack was mounted on the island of Kyushu. The second phase, Operation Coronet, called for landings on Honshu and an advance toward Tokyo. After the resistance that had been seen on Iwo Jima and Okinawa, American military planners estimated that American losses for the complete strategy would be approximately 1,000,000 men. They were unaware of the deteriorating morale of the Japanese people and were basing their figures on the strength of the defenses in the area. There were at least 2,300,000 Japanese regular troops and with the intervention of civilian volunteers it was estimated

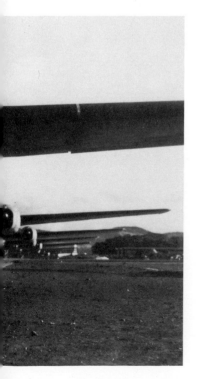

Left: Boeing B-29 Super-fortress bombers prepare to take off from an airfield in the Marianas for a raid on a target in the Japanese Home Islands. Japanese cities were particularly vulnerable to incendiary bombing attacks because of the wood and paper construction of many of the houses.
Above left: President Truman seen during a broadcast soon after Roosevelt's death. Truman was attending the Potsdam conference with Churchill and Stalin when he was told that the atomic bomb had been successfully tested.
Above right: Admirals Nimitz (left) and Fraser after the Japanese surrender. Fraser commanded the British Pacific Fleet which took part in the Okinawa campaign and the attacks on Japan which followed.

that the defensive strength could swell to nearly 30,000,000. Although the figures were staggering the strategists realized that the majority would be unarmed civilians. This did not matter however as they could try to overwhelm the American forces by sheer weight of numbers.

In the planning efforts it was decided that some 750,000 men would participate in Operation Olympic while MacArthur, who preferred to use his own code-name for the invasion of Honshu, Operation Downfall, had a total of 5,000,000 Allied troops under his command. Support for the operations would definitely have been completely in favor of the United States. There were 10,000 American aircraft scheduled to participate and although it was estimated that the Japanese might have an equal number, they were certainly not skilled aircrews. The most serious threat would be the Kamikaze. Japanese naval power was virtually non-existent. There were only 19 Japanese destroyers known to be protecting the Home Islands, though it was believed that several thousand small craft might be equipped for suicidal missions as had been seen at Okinawa. The American and Allied navies included 20 aircraft carriers, nine battleships, 22 cruisers and more than 80 destroyers for Operation Olympic alone.

After the plans and possibilities were painstakingly calculated they were laid before President Truman. He immediately disapproved of them. The preparations that needed to be made extended the invasion date for the island of Honshu to 1 March 1946, though Operation Olympic could be launched as early as November 1945. He decided that another strategy had to be devised. The means to that strategy were soon to be placed in his hands. The Manhattan Project

had been completed and the first test made on 16 July. Two atomic bombs now existed. Truman was approached with the idea of using these weapons rather than attempt to invade Japan. Not only would the bombs demonstrate to the Japanese that the United States could bring unprecedented destruction to bear but they would save the lives of perhaps 1,000,000 Allied soldiers and countless Japanese. On 1 June 1945 when the Interim Committee had reported on the Manhattan Project, they had made three recommendations. First, that the weapons should be used against Japan as soon as possible; second, that the targets should be locations of both industrial and civilian concentrations; and third and most important, that the weapon should be used without warning. The reason given for the final recommendation was that the planners were afraid that if the Japanese knew that such a bomb was to be dropped they might move Allied prisoners of war into the drop site. It was also feared that if the United States made too great an issue of its ultimate weapon and it did not work, the failure could cause complications which would have a serious effect on America's standing in the world.

Full preparation had been made for the use of the atomic bomb. The crew which had been chosen to carry out the mission had been in training since November 1944 and the possible city targets had been listed. Of the 10 possible targets the seventh largest Japanese city, Hiroshima, headed the list, and the fourth on the list, Nagasaki, was chosen also.

On 26 July 1945 the United States, Great Britain

Above right: The ruins of Hiroshima after the atomic attack.
Below left: The mushroom cloud rises over Nagasaki.
Below: Colonel Tibbets poses in front of the *Enola* Gay.

and China jointly called on the Japanese government to surrender unconditionally. The Japanese war leaders refused. On 6 August 1945 three American bombers, one of which carried the atomic bomb while the other two carried cameras and scientific equipment, left Tinian in the Marianas. At 0811 hours the aircraft circled above Hiroshima, and the *Enola Gay*, piloted by Colonel Paul Tibbets, dropped the first atomic bomb. Within moments 80 percent of the buildings in the city were reduced to rubble. The Japanese government would later release figures which suggested that 71,000 people were killed with an equal number injured. After the war American medical teams raised that latter figure to 200,000 who suffered from the lingering effects of radiation.

Although the bomb's effects were devastating Japanese officials who immediately inspected the site did not seem to think that the destruction was unusual, considering the effects of the American raids on Tokyo. At first they believed that the huge destruction in Hiroshima was caused by a massive air raid not just one aircraft. When Japan still refused to surrender Truman ordered the second bomb dropped. On 9 August the second atomic bomb was detonated at Nagasaki. Again Japanese officials investigating the bombing found nothing unusual but word was beginning to reach them about the unusual injuries being found at Hiroshima. Strange burns and serious illness, which would be confirmed as radiation effects, were

baffling the doctors. It was finally accepted that some terrible new weapon did in fact exist. The following day the Japanese government sued for peace, ordering all Japanese forces to lay down their arms and surrender.

On 14 August President Truman addressed the American people, announcing that the Japanese had unconditionally surrendered. The final surrender was signed on 2 September on the quarterdeck of the battleship *Missouri* in Tokyo Bay. General Douglas MacArthur presided over the event. In the days ahead he would rule Japan benevolently and become the most instrumental force in the reconstruction and redirection of the country.

The war was over. In the Pacific it had been fought in two waves: the initial Japanese surge of expansion and the reactive American drive to complete victory. It had been a total war. Although the United States was caught unprepared for war, its resources and the grim determination of the American people in a time of crisis carried the nation to ultimate victory. The will and sacrifice of the men who fought in the Pacific deserve the highest recognition, as does the skill and caliber of the officers and commanders under whom they served. The United States had again proven its claim to recognition as a major world power but perhaps most important, the Pacific conflict will be remembered as the battleground which launched the world into the Atomic Age.

INDEX

Adak Island, 32
Admiralty Islands, attack on, 37
Akagi, 21, 23
Aleutian Islands, 20–24, 30, 32–33, 35
Amchitka Island, 32
Arizona, 11
Arnold, General Henry, 17
American Volunteer Group (AVG), 30–31

B-17 bomber, 10, *13*
B-25 bomber, 17, *21*
B-29 bomber, *31*, 38, 46, 54, 57, 61
Bataan Death March, 16
Bloody Ridge, Battle of, 29
Bougainville Island, Battle of, 36–37, *37*
Buckner, General Simon B, 57–58
Bunker Hill, 44, 58
Burma, 31–32, 35

Caroline Islands, 41–42, 47
Cates, General Clifton B, 54
Chennault, Colonel Claire, 30, *31*, 32
Chiang Kai-shek, 30–31
China, 6–9, 17, 30–32, 61, 63
Chinese Air Force, 30
   Nationalist Army, 31
Chiyoda, 45
Churchill, Winston, 34–35
Clark airfield, 16, 52–53
Coral Sea, Battle of the, 18–19, 20, 24–25, 38
Corregidor, 16, 53

Dauntless dive bomber, *17*, *19*, *23*, *27*, *38*
Doolittle, Colonel JH, 17
Doolittle Raid on Tokyo, 17–18, 20, *21*
Doorman, Admiral Karl, 17
Downes, *10*, 48
Dutch East Indies, 15, 42, 47

Enola Gay, 46, *62*, 63
Enterprise, 21, 23, 24–25, *27*, *28*, 29, 58
Erskine, General Graves B, 54

Fletcher, Admiral Frank J, 18–19, *19*, 25, 27
Flying Tigers, 30–31
Formosa, 16, 51

Gambier Bay, 49
Geiger, General Roy, 57
Gilbert Islands, 41
Great Marianas Turkey Shoot, 44
Griswold, General Oscar, 52–53
Guadalcanal, Battle of, *24*, 24–29, *25*, 34, 36
Guam, Battle for, 15, 30, 44–46

Hall, General Charles P, 53
Halsey, Admiral William F, 30, *35*, 35, 36–37,
   38, 42, 47–48, 51
Haruna, 45
Hawaiian Islands, 20, 25
Henderson Field, 26–28
Hiroshima, 46, *62*, 62–63
Hiryu, 21, 23
Hiyo, 45
Hodge, General John R, 57
Hoel, 49
Hornet, 17, *21*, 21, 24, 28
Houston, 17

Ichiki, Colonel, 27
India, 31, 32, 35
Intelligence, American, 18, 22, 33, 36, 41,
   54–55
   Japanese, 21–22
Intrepid, 39
Isolationist policy, 6, 8
Iwo Jima, invasion of, *54*, 54–60, *55*, *57*

Japanese Air Force, 37, 54
   Army, 31, 57–58
   Expansion program, 9, 18, 29–30

Fourteenth Army, 16
Government, 30, 62
Home Islands, 35, 42, 50–51, 54, 62
Imperial Command, 17, 36, 42, 57, 61
Navy, 9–10, 15, 17–29, 36–37, 44–46, 50, 62
Java Sea, Battle of, 17
Johnston, 49
Juneau, 27

Kaga, 21, 23
Kamikaze, 50, *51*, *52*–54, 57–58, 62
Kenney, General George, 51
Kimmel, Admiral Husband E, 9, 9–11
King, Admiral Ernest J, *17*, 17, 35, 38, 41
Kinkaid, Admiral Thomas C, *33*, 50, 51, *52*
Kiska Island, 32–33
Krueger, General Walter, 50, 51
Kumano, 49
Kurita, Admiral, 48–49

Lanphier, Captain TG, 36
LeMay, General Curtis, 61
Leyte Gulf, Battle of, *47*, 47–48
Lexington, 18–19, *19*
Liscombe Bay, 41
Luzon, invasion of, 47, 51–53

MacArthur, General Douglas, 16, 25, 30, *34*,
   34–38, 42, 47–48, 51–53, 62
McMorris, Admiral Alexander, 32
Makin, assault on, 41
Manchurian Incident, 30
Marianas Islands, 42–47, 60
Marshall, General George, 16
Marshall Islands, 41–42
Maya, 45
Merrill, General Frank, 32
Midway, Battle of, 20–24, *21*, 25, 32, 38, 44
Mindoro, 47, 51
Missouri, 41
Mitscher, Admiral Marc A, 42–48, *46*, 58
Morale, 16, 17, 33, 36, 50, 56, 61

Nagasaki, 62, *62*
Nagumo, Admiral, 10
Nazi Germany, 30, 34
Neutrality Laws and policy, 7–8
New Guinea Campaign, 36, 42
Nimitz, Admiral Chester, *17*, 17, 22–25, 30, 35,
   38–42, *42*, 54, 60, 61
Nishimura, Admiral, 47
North Carolina, 27, 28

Oahu Island, attack on, 10–11
Oaklahoma, 11
Okinawa, invasion of, 56, 57–58, *59*, 62
Oldendorf, Admiral Jesse B, 47, *56*
Operation Cartwheel, 35
   Coronet, 61
   Downfall, 62
   Flintlock, 42
   Olympic, 61–62
Ozawa, Admiral, *42*, 42–46

P-38 fighter, 36
P-40 fighter, *13*, *33*
P-51 fighter, 57
Panama Conference, 8
Panay, *8*, 8
Pearl Harbor, 6, *7*, 9–16, *13*, *14*, 18, 22, 26, 38
Philippines, 9, 15–17, 30, 34–35, 37, 42, 47,
   51–53
Philippine Sea, Battle of the, *42*, 42–46, *43*, *46*
Port Moresby, 18, 24–25, 27, 36
Pownall, Admiral Charles A, 41
Propaganda, 16–17, 61

Rabaul, 26–27, 35–37, 42
Rockey, General Keller E, 54
Roosevelt, Franklin, 6, 6–9, 12, 16, 30, 34, 51,
   60

Saipan, attack on, 44–46
Samar Island, Battle of, 49–50
Samuel B Roberts, 49
Santa Cruz, Battle of, 28, *29*
Saratoga, 25, 27, 28

Shepherd, General Lemuel C, *59*
Shimada, Admiral, *6*
Shoho, 18
Shokaku, 18–19, 27, 44–45
Singapore, 15
Slot, the, 26–28
Smith, General Holland, 41–54
Solomon Islands Campaign, 25–29, 35–37, 42
Soryu, 21, 23
Sprague, Admiral CF, 48–49
Spruance, Admiral Raymond A, 41, *42*, 42–46,
   56, 57
Stilwell, General, 31, *32*, 35
Submarines, 20–21, 44, 46, 48, 61
Sullivan brothers, 27
Swift, General Innis P, 52

Taiho, 44–45
Tarawa Atoll, Battle for, 41
Tennessee, 56
Tibbets, Colonel Paul, *62*, 63
Tokyo, 17–18, 20, 61
'Tokyo Express', 29
Trident Conference, 34–35
Truk, 42
Truman, Harry S, *60*, 60, 62
Tulagi, assault on, 25–26
Turner, Admiral Kelly, 25, 26, 41, *42*

US Air Corps, 31
   Tenth Air Force, 31
US Army, 36
US Congress, 8, 12
US Marines, *25*, 25–29, *28*, 35–46, *37*, *40*, *43*,
   46, *54*, 54–58, *59*
US Navy, 8, 12, 17, 20–23, 25–26, 32–33, 36,
   38–44, 62
   Fifth Fleet, 41, 45–46
   special service fleets, 40–41
USSR, 8, 30

Vandegrift, General Alexander, 25

Wake Island, 15, 30
Wainwright, General Jonathan, 16
Wasp, 25, 28
Wasp (second of same name), 44
West Virginia, *10*, 11
Wingate, General Orde, 32

Yamamoto, Admiral, 6, *6*, 12, 20–24, 36
Yamato, 58
Yorktown, 18–19, 20, *21*, 23

Zero fighters, 38, *39*
Zuikaku, 18, 27, 45

Page references in italics refer to illustrations.

Acknowledgements

The author would like to thank Adrian
Hodgkins who designed this book, Penny
Murphy who compiled the index and Richard
Natkiel who drew the maps. The following
agencies kindly supplied the illustrations.

Bison Picture Library: 6 left, 13 top, 32 bottom
Robert Hunt Library: 62 left, 63
Imperial War Museum: 20 bottom, 46
National Archives (US): 1, 2–3, 7 bottom,
   10–11 both, 14–15, 17 both, 18, 19 all three,
   20 top, 21, 24–25, 25, 26, 26–27, 28 both, 29
   top, 34–35, 37 top right and bottom, 38, 39
   center and bottom, 40 top, 42 center, 44–45,
   45, 47, 48 both, 49, 50–51 top, 52, 57 both, 60
National Maritime Museum (UK): 61
US Air Force: 7 top, 12 top, 13 bottom, 31
   both, 32 top, 33 right, 39 top, 50–51 bottom,
   53, 60–61, 62 right
US Army: 34 top, 50
US Marines: 4–5, 24 bottom, 29 bottom, 37
   top left, 40 bottom, 43, 55 top left and
   bottom, 56 both, 59 all four
US Naval Institute, Annapolis: 55 top right
US Navy: 6 center and right, 8–9 all three, 12
   bottom, 16, 22–23 all three, 27, 33 left, 35,
   42 left and right.